FORTUNE-TELLING BY CARDS

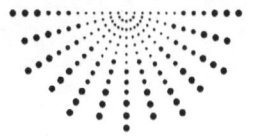

PROFESSOR P. R. S. FOLI

CONTENTS

Introduction   1

CHAPTER I. How we got our Pack of Cards   3
Where do they come from?—The Romany Folk—Were they made in Europe?—Suits and signs—The power of cards—Their charm and interest—Necessity for sympathy—Value of Cartomancy.

CHAPTER II. What the Individual Cards Signify   9
Two systems—The English method—The foreign—Significations of the cards—Hearts—Diamonds—Clubs—Spades—A short table—Mystic meanings.

CHAPTER III. The Selected Pack of Thirty-two Cards   15
Reduced pack generally used—How to indicate reversed cards—Meaning of Hearts—Diamonds—Clubs—Spades.

CHAPTER IV. The Signification of Quartettes, Triplets, and Pairs   18
Combinations of court cards—Combinations of plain cards—Various cards read together—General meaning of the several suits—Some lesser points to notice.

CHAPTER V.   23
What the Cards can Tell of the Past, the Present, and the Future A simple method—What the cards say—The present—The future.

CHAPTER VI. Your Fortune in Twenty-one Cards   27
A reduced pack—An example—The three packs—The surprise.

CHAPTER VII. Combination of Sevens   33
A method with selected cards—General rules—How to proceed—Reading of the cards—Signification of cards—Some combinations—A typical example—Further inquiries—The seven packs.

CHAPTER VIII. Another Method   41
General outline—Signification of cards—How to consult the cards—An illustration—Its reading.

CHAPTER IX. A French Method   46
French system—The reading—An example.

CHAPTER X. The Grand Star   50
The number of cards may vary—The method—The reading in pairs—Diagram of the Grand Star—An example.

CHAPTER XI. Important Questions   54
How to answer them—Specimen questions—Cupid and Venus at work.

CHAPTER XII. How They Tell Fortunes in Italy   60
Italian method—An example—Notice the groups—How the pairs work out—The five packs.

CHAPTER XIII. The Master Method — 65
Knowledge is power — Four twos added to the usual pack — The thirty-six squares and their significance — Tendencies of the suits.

CHAPTER XIV. Signification of Suits in the Master Method — 79
Court cards — Plain cards — An example of the Master Method.

CHAPTER XV. Combination of Nines — 88
How to work it — An example — The First Reading — The Second Reading — The Third Reading

CHAPTER XVI. Your Heart's Desire — 92
The wish with fifteen cards — Another way — The wish with thirty-two cards — What the four aces tell — The wish in seven packs — The wish card again.

CHAPTER XVII. A Rhyming Divination — 97
Diamonds — Hearts — Spades — Clubs.

CHAPTER XVIII. The Tarots — 105
Derivation of name — Remote origin — The great Etteilla.

CHAPTER XIX. Etteilla's Method — 108
The Major Arcana — The Minor Arcana — General rules — The second deal — The third deal or great figure — The fourth deal.

INTRODUCTION

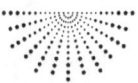

"THIS goddess Fortune frustrates, single-handed, the plans of a hundred learned men." In this saying the Latin author has given us the key to all the restless striving to search out the Unknown and the Unknowable which marks our own age, just as it has marked previous periods in history which we are apt to look back upon as being but little removed from the dark ages.

Of all the methods by which men and women seek to penetrate into the mysteries of Fate and Futurity, Cartomancy is one that can claim the distinction of having swayed the human mind from prehistoric times right down to this twentieth century of ours.

It may be that this book will fall into the hands of those who agree with the words of L'Estrange: "There needs no more than impudence on the one side and a superstitious credulity on the other to the setting up of a Fortune-teller." This attitude of cynical superiority is sometimes genuine, but in many cases if we could read what lies beneath the surface we should find that it is but a cloak worn to conceal a lurking fear, an almost irritated condition of mind, born of a half-confessed faith in the power at which it is so easy to scoff.

There is a vein of superstition in every human heart, and many men who have played a great part in the world's history have not been ashamed to seek help from occultists, when the tangle of life seemed too involved for them to unravel with the ordinary means at their disposal.

The pages of history are full of the penalties meted out by kings and rulers to those who were accused of working evil spells upon them. It needs but to mention the names of Wallenstein, Murat, King of Naples; Bernadotte, afterwards King of Sweden; and the merciless Robespierre, as types of a vast number over whom the fascinations of Astrology and Cartomancy, which are so closely allied, have cast their witching spell.

Pope treats the cards as sentient entities:

> *"The king, unseen,*
> *Lurked in her hand and mourned his captive queen."*

While in another passage he says:

> *"Soon as she spreads her cards th' aerial guard*
> *Descend and sit on each important card."*

In the following pages we have given information that will, we hope, afford interest and amusement to many. We have not dwelt on the gift of prophecy, or on the power of second sight claimed by apostles of the occult. We would in no case obtrude the subject of Cartomancy upon the notice of those whose susceptibilities would be wounded, or whose sense of right and wrong would be outraged by the practice, and we have ventured to speak a word of warning to the morbidly minded.

We give this method of Fortune-telling for what it is worth. It may be either a pastime seasoned with a flavour of mystery, a study in the weird ways of coincidence, or a test of skill quickened by intuition. We would have all our readers amused and interested, but none saddened or enslaved by it.

CHAPTER I. HOW WE GOT OUR PACK OF CARDS

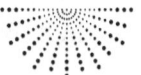

WHERE DO THEY COME FROM?—THE ROMANY FOLK—WERE THEY MADE IN EUROPE?—SUITS AND SIGNS—THE POWER OF CARDS—THEIR CHARM AND INTEREST—NECESSITY FOR SYMPATHY—VALUE OF CARTOMANCY.

Where do They Come From?

WHEN we take up an ordinary pack of cards to deal them out for a rubber, or to lay them down in the careful deliberation of Patience, or when we watch them being used as the inexplicable instruments of a something that, with a feeling akin to superstitious dread, we prefer to call coincidence, we do not often stop to think of the varied and eventful history represented by those smooth, highly-glazed playthings.

The actual and authentic history of playing cards only goes back about five hundred years, and various theories have been mooted as to the source from which Europe obtained them. It is an established fact that in past ages many eastern peoples, notably those of India, China, and Chaldea, possessed cards which differed materially both in use and design from those known in the West at a later date. It is impossible to trace these prehistoric beginnings of card-lore, but there seems little doubt that the Wise Men of eastern lands regarded their cards with none of the contempt usually bestowed upon them in the West. They held them in high esteem as mediums for the partial revelation of the Unknowable, and included them as a part of their mystic lore.

The Romany Folk.

It is thought by many that we owe our cards to the gipsies, who are supposed to have been the offspring of a low caste of Hindus, and who, driven from their own land, found their way, as fugitives, through Western Asia into Egypt, and from Northern Africa into Europe. It is certain that all kinds of fortune-telling, whether by Cartomancy or whatever method, are inseparably connected with that curious, fascinating, highly gifted and elusive people. They excelled in music and ail mechanical pursuits; they could learn a language, or distinguish themselves in metal work, with equal ease; but they had to live more or less on the defensive, as very children of Ishmael, and years of persecution only deepened their craftiness, sharpened their intuition, and rendered them more keen to assert their mysterious power over those who oppressed and yet inwardly feared them.

These Romany folk have preserved intact the ancient lore of the East, while incredulous Europe has turned the sacred pages of divination from the book of fate into mere instruments of amusement, and a vehicle for winning or losing money. The gipsy remains a past master in the art of Cartomancy, and though we may scoff, there are very few amongst us who do not feel a sense of disquietude when brought face to face with an instance of her uncanny power. We can afford to laugh when the sun of our lives is shining brightly and all is well in mind and body, but there come dark days in the lives of all, and then some are impelled to seek the aid of these weird sons and daughters of an unknown land.

By many, perhaps by the majority, this inexplicable gift has been vulgarised and debased to a mere means of extorting money from the ignorant and the credulous; but by some it is still held as a sacred faith —possibly no more superstitious than some forms of unenlightened or perverted Christianity.

Were They Made in Europe?

Another theory separates the cards of the West entirely from those of the East, and holds that the western were originally made in Europe. This is as it may be. A writer of the latter part of the fifteenth century says that cards were first known at Viterbo in 1379, and that they had been introduced by the Saracens, who, with the Arabs and Moors, have the credit of planting the seeds of Cartomancy in Spain. It is certain that at first cards were called by the name *naibi;* and the Hebrew and Arabic words, *Nabi, naba, nabaa,* signify "to foretell." It is also widely believed that the idea of playing games with cards was an after-thought, and that their original purpose was for the practice of divination.

The earliest cards were the Tarots, of which we speak in another chapter, and it is supposed that some one had the bright idea of adding the numeral to the symbolical cards, so as to play games with them. This addition was made about the middle of the fourteenth century, and at the beginning of the fifteenth century there was a pack in Venice composed of seventy-eight cards, twenty-two symbols and fifty-six numerals; with four *coat* (court) cards, king, queen, chevalier, and valet, and ten *point* or pip cards to each suit. The fifty-six numerals were subsequently reduced to the present number, fifty-two, by the rejection of one of the picture cards.

The Spaniards discourteously abolished the queens, but the French, true to their reputation, kept the dame and rejected the chevalier. The early German packs were the same as the French, but the queens again were cast out in favour of a superior knave called the *Obermann.* England accepted the Spanish or French pack as she found it.

Suits and Signs.

There have always been four suits, but there have been many changes in the signs used to mark them. The original quartette were:— Cups, supposed to be emblematical of Faith; Money, representing Charity; Swords, figuring Justice; and Clubs, typical of Fortitude. These signs are still retained in the Tarots, and in Italian and Spanish cards. Old German packs have bells, hearts, leaves, and acorns; and during the fifteenth century the French adopted spades (*pique*), hearts, clubs (*trèfle*), and diamonds.

There is some difficulty in tracing how we come by the word spade in this connection. It has been thought to be a corruption of the Italian word spade, meaning swords. It is not known why the French should have called this suit *pique.* Our suit of clubs is known by the French as *trèfle,* from their drawing the sign like the trefoil; and the Germans call it *Eichel* from its resemblance to an acorn. Our name is supposed to show Italian influence, though where the connection between the word *bastoni* and our sign is to be found, I am at a loss to say. The heart sign needs no explanation, and is found in French, German, and English packs. It corresponds to the Spanish and Italian sign of cups. By some curious evolution the signs of money and bells were squared into the French *carreaux*, our diamonds.

Many of the packs used in the fourteenth century were of the most artistic and costly nature, and in some cases the court cards were drawn so as to represent historic characters.

The Power of Cards.

Fierce controversies have ranged round these apparently simple pieces of glazed pasteboard. They have exercised such an irresistible fascination upon the minds of men and women of all grades and ages that others have risen in wild revolt against this power, which had no attraction for them, and which they longed to crush out of existence. There are still those amongst us who will not have a card in the house, and who, even if they do not use it, acquiesce in the term "the Devil's books," which has been applied to the pack.

With their use for gambling purposes we have nothing to do here. As the instruments of Cartomancy we give them our respectful consideration. We would urge those of a morbid and unhealthy turn of mind to beware of letting this practice take too strong a hold upon them. No reasonable being need be ashamed of confessing a certain fear of the Unseen and the Unknowable; but, on the other hand, no sane person would take a pack of cards as the rule and guide of life, the final court of appeal in any matters of moment.

Their Charm and Interest.

There is much amusement to be derived from the study of Cartomancy, and it is not to be denied that there are certain persons who appear to have the power of making the meaning of the cards vivid and convincing, while in the hands of others there seems neither rhyme nor reason in their manipulation of the most carefully shuffled pack. We may call things by what name we will, but strange coincidences meet us at every turn, and now and then there seems but the thinnest veil between us and the Future, which is so sedulously hidden from us.

There has been a great revival of interest in all matters relating to occultism in the immediate past, and if we are to believe what we read and hear, educated men and women of to-day are going to have their fortunes told as eagerly as did the great men and famous women of France during the stormy period of the Revolution, and under the sway of the great Napoleon himself. Many curious and convincing instances of accurate foreshadowing of future events are told with regard to the famous Mademoiselle Lenormand, and other cartomancers who held undisputed sway over the minds of society at a time when credulity was supposed to have been cast off with the trammels of a worn-out creed.

So when the fortune-tellers of the twentieth century take a pack of cards and proceed to read the mysteries revealed therein, they are following the example of the wise men of Chaldea, Egypt, and China, the Flowery Land of the East, to say nothing of their European predecessors.

Divination by cards, therefore, is of great antiquity and of world-wide popularity. Formerly it was combined with a knowledge of astrology; but now it is considered sufficient to follow the general rules laid down by one or two famous cartomancers, and to rely on intuition and experience for details.

Necessity for Sympathy.

Any one with the slightest knowledge of occultism is aware that sympathy with the inquirer or subject is essential.

It is true that cold reason tells us that the cards are pieces of pasteboard and nothing more, and that it is the height of absurdity to expect any revelation; yet, in dealing with them, human sympathy may discern something of our perplexities, and all unconsciously set our feet on the right path.

Value of Cartomancy.

In the following pages there are several methods of divination by cards. Any one observing the rules can learn the signification of the cards, and while a study of the combinations they resolve into in the hands of different people will always provide a fund of amusement, it may also—in all seriousness I say it—inspire hope in the place of despair, assuage sorrow, and send the inquirer away comforted; surely no insignificant result.

CHAPTER II. WHAT THE INDIVIDUAL CARDS SIGNIFY

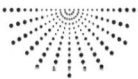

TWO SYSTEMS—THE ENGLISH METHOD—
THE FOREIGN—SIGNIFICATIONS OF THE
CARDS—HEARTS—DIAMONDS—CLUBS—
SPADES—A SHORT TABLE—MYSTIC
MEANINGS.

Two Systems.

THERE are two separate systems of explaining the cards individually: one which makes use of the whole pack of fifty-two cards, and another which only employs thirty-two, throwing out the plain cards under seven of each suit.

The English Method.

The former plan is sometimes spoken of as the English method, and in it we do not find mention of reversed cards bearing a different meaning from those which come out in the ordinary way. This is probably to be explained by the fact that the larger number in use affords sufficient shades of meaning, and the task of remembering one hundred and four significations would be too heavy for many minds.

The Foreign.

In the latter system, which is more distinctly traceable to foreign sources, we get the signification of each card modified, or even contradicted, by its position being upright or the reverse.

The following definitions apply to the use of the whole pack, and have been worked up from both ancient and modern sources of information. It must always be borne in mind that the reading of the cards has come down to us through many ages, has been passed on to us through count less hands and in varied tongues. Cartomancy has travelled from the East to the West, from the South to the North, and its secrets have been, for the most part, jealously preserved by oral tradition among its weird and fascinating votaries.

Significations of the Cards.

The following definitions are based upon one of the oldest authorities dealing with the subject, and have been amplified by some of the more modern meanings now in vogue,

HEARTS.

Ace.—An important card, whose meaning is affected by its environment. Among hearts it implies love, friendship, and affection; with diamonds, money and news of distant friends; with clubs, festivities, and social or domestic rejoicing; with, spades, disagreements, misunderstandings, contention, or misfortune; individually, it stands for the house.

King.—A good-hearted man, with strong affections, emotional, and given to rash judgments, possessing more zeal than discretion.

Queen.—A fair woman, loving and lovable, domesticated, prudent, and faithful.

Knave.—Not endowed with any sex. Sometimes taken as Cupid; also as the best friend of the inquirer, or as a fair person's thoughts. The cards on either side of the knave are indicative of the good or bad nature of its intentions.

Ten.—A sign of good fortune. It implies a good heart, happiness, and the prospect of a large family. It counteracts bad cards and confirms good ones in its vicinity.

Nine.—The wish card. It is the sign of riches, and of high social position accompanied by influence and esteem. It may be affected by the neighbourhood of bad cards.

Eight.—The pleasures of the table, convivial society. Another meaning implies love and marriage.

Seven.—A faithless, inconstant friend who may prove an enemy.

Six.—A confiding nature, liberal, open-handed, and an easy prey for swindlers; courtship, and a possible proposal.

Five.—Causeless jealousy in a person of weak, unsettled character.

Four.—One who has remained single till middle life from being too hard to please.

Three.—A warning card as to the possible results of the inquirer's own want of prudence and tact.

Deuce.—Prosperity and success in a measure dependent on the surrounding cards; endearments and wedding bells.

DIAMONDS.

Ace.—A ring or paper money.

King.—A fair man, with violent temper, and a vindictive, obstinate turn of mind.

Queen.—A fair woman, given to flirtation, fond of society and admiration.

Knave.—A near relative who puts his own interests first, is self-opinionated, easily offended, and not always quite straight. It may mean a fair person's thoughts.

Ten.—Plenty of money, a husband or wife from the country, and several children.

Nine.—This card is influenced by the one accompanying it; if the latter be a court card, the person referred to will have his capacities discounted by a restless, wandering disposition. It may imply a surprise connected with money, or if in conjunction with the eight of spades it signifies cross swords.

Eight.—A marriage late in life, which will probably be somewhat chequered.

Seven.—This card has various meanings. It enjoins the need for careful action. It may imply a decrease of prosperity. Another reading connects it with uncharitable tongues.

Six.—An early marriage and speedy widowhood. A warning with regard to second marriage is also included.

Five.—To young married people this portends good children. In a general way it means unexpected news, or success in business enterprises.

Four.—Breach of confidence. Troubles caused by inconstant friends, vexations and disagreeables.

Three.—Legal and domestic quarrels, and probable un-Sappiness caused by wife's or husband's temper.

Deuce.—An unsatisfactory love affair, awakening opposition from relatives or friends.

CLUBS.

Ace.—Wealth, a peaceful home, industry, and general prosperity.

King.—A dark man of upright, high-minded nature. calculated to make an excellent husband, faithful and true in his affections.

Queen.—A dark woman, with a trustful, affectionate disposition, with great charm for the opposite sex, and susceptible to male attractions.

Knave.—A generous, trusty friend, who will take trouble on behalf of the inquirer. It may also mean a dark man's thoughts.

Ten.—Riches suddenly acquired, probably through the death of a relation or friend.

Nine.—Friction through opposition to the wishes of friends.

Eight.—Love of money, and a passion for speculating.

Seven.—Great happiness and good fortune. If troubles come they will be caused by one of the opposite sex to the inquirer.

Six.—Success in business both for self and children.

Five.—An advantageous marriage.

Four.—A warning against falsehood and double-dealing.

Three.—Two or possibly three marriages, with money.

Deuce.—Care is needed to avert disappointment, and to avoid opposition.

SPADES.

Ace.—It may concern love affairs, or convey a warning that troubles await the inquirer through bad speculations or ill-chosen friends.

King.—A dark man. Ambitious and successful in the higher walks of life.

Queen.—A widow, of malicious and unscrupulous nature, fond of scandal and open to bribes.

Knave.—A well-meaning, inert person, unready in action though kindly in thought.

Ten.—An evil omen; grief or imprisonment. Has power to detract from the good signified by cards near it.

Nine.—An ill-fated card, meaning sickness, losses, troubles, and family dissensions.

Eight.—A warning with regard to any enterprise in hand, This card close to the inquirer means evil; also opposition from friends.

Seven.—Sorrow caused by the loss of a dear friend. Six.—Hard work brings wealth and rest after toil. Five.—Bad temper and a tendency to interfere in the inquirer, but happiness to be found in the chosen wife or husband.

Four.—Illness and the need for great attention to business.

Three.—A marriage that will be marred by the inconstancy of the inquirer's wife or husband; or a journey.

Deuce.—A removal, or possibly death.

In connection with the foregoing detailed explanation of the meanings of each card in an ordinary pack, we append a short table, which may be studied either separately or with the preceding definitions. It gives at a glance certain broad outlines, which may be of use to one who wishes to acquire the art of reading a card directly it is placed before the eye:

Mystic Meanings.

There is fascination in certain calculations, and the following figures are not without a deep interest to those attracted by the study of Cartomancy.

The fifty-two cards in the pack correspond with the fifty-two weeks in the year.

The thirteen cards in each suit symbolise the thirteen lunar months, and the thirteen weeks in each quarter.

There are four suits, as there are four seasons in the year. There are twelve court cards in the pack, just as there are twelve calendar months and twelve signs of the Zodiac.

A Short Table.

PRUDENCE.	WEALTH.	REJOICING.	EARLY MARRIAGE.
Ace of clubs.	9 of hearts.	8 of hearts.	2 of clubs.
6 of spades.	2 „ „		6 „ diamonds.
	7 „ clubs.		3 „ clubs.
	10 „ diamonds.		5 „ clubs.
	10 „ clubs.		
CREDULITY.	**JEALOUSY.**	**UNFAITHFULNESS.**	**LATE MARRIAGE.**
6 of hearts.	5 of hearts.	King of diamonds.	8 of diamonds
		4 of diamonds.	4 „ clubs.
		3 „ clubs.	
		7 „ hearts.	
PROSPERITY.	**DISCRETION NEEDED.**	**PRESAGE MISFORTUNE.**	
10 of hearts.	3 of hearts.	10 of spades.	
2 „ „	7 „ diamonds.	9 „ „	
7 „ clubs.	2 „ „	8 „ „	
6 „ „	2 „ clubs.	7 „ „	
	4 „ spades.	3 „ „	
		2 „ „	
		3 „ diamonds.	
		9 „ clubs.	

A Curious Calculation.

- Number of pips on the plain cards of the four suit: 220
- „   „   „ court   „   „: 12
- Twelve court cards, counted as 10 each: 120
- Number of cards in each suit: 13
- Equal to the number of days in the year: 365

CHAPTER III. THE SELECTED PACK OF THIRTY-TWO CARDS

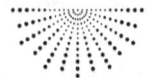

REDUCED PACK GENERALLY USED—HOW TO INDICATE REVERSED CARDS—MEANING OF HEARTS—DIAMONDS—CLUBS—SPADES.

Reduced Pack Generally Used.

THE practice of using only thirty-two cards in telling fortune is very general, especially in those systems which have been adopted from or based upon a foreign source. We here give the definitions used in these methods, as they differ in certain respects from those given with the entire pack of fifty-two cards. Special care must be taken when using the selected pack to notice which way the cards come out upon the table, whether upright or reversed, as the meanings of the two positions may be diametrically opposed.

How to Indicate Reversed Cards.

In former days it was easier to distinguish between the top and the bottom of a card, but now that they are practically made reversible, with a few exceptions, it is necessary to mark the cards that are to be used for fortune-telling in such a way as to enable the dealer to say at a glance whether the card is reversed or not. These marks should be made before the pack has been used, and need not be altered if the cards are kept solely for this purpose.

In the following pages this selected pack is required for several methods, and in the case of the Master Method it is augmented by the four twos taken from the excluded cards.

Meaning of the Hearts.

Ace.—A love letter, good news; reversed, a removal or a visit from a friend.

King.—Fair man of generous disposition; reversed, a disappointing person.

Queen.—Fair, good-natured woman; reversed, she has had an unhappy love affair.

Knave.—A young bachelor devoted to enjoyment; reversed, a military lover with a grievance.

Ten.—Antidote to bad cards; happiness and success; reversed, passing worries.

Nine.—The wish card, good luck; reversed, short sorrow.

Eight.—Thoughts of marriage, affections of a fair person; reversed, unresponsiveness.

Seven.—Calm content; reversed, boredom, satiety.

Meaning of the Diamonds.

Ace.—A letter, an offer of marriage; reversed, evil tidings.

King.—A very fair or white-haired man, a soldier by profession, and of a deceitful turn of mind; reversed, a treacherous schemer.

Queen.—A fair woman, given to gossip and wanting in refinement; reversed, rather a spiteful flirt.

Knave.—Subordinate official, who is untrustworthy; reversed, a mischief-maker.

Ten.—Travelling or a removal; reversed, ill-luck will attend the step.

Nine.—Vexation, hindrances; reversed, domestic wrangling, or disagreement between lovers.

Eight.—Love passages; reversed, blighted affections. *Seven.*—Unkindly chat cynicism; reversed, stupid and unfounded slander.

Meaning of the Clubs.

Ace.—Good luck, letters or papers relating to money, pleasant tidings; reversed, short-lived happiness, a tiresome correspondence.

King.—A dark man, warm-hearted and true as a friend, straight in his dealings; reversed, good intentions frustrated.

Queen.—A dark woman, loving but hasty, and bearing no malice; reversed, harassed by jealousy.

Knave.—A ready-witted young man, clever at his work and ardent in his love; reversed, irresponsible and fickle.

Ten.—Prosperity and luxury; reversed, a sea voyage.

Nine.—An unlooked-for inheritance, money acquired under a will; reversed, a small, friendly gift.

Eight.—Love of a dark man or woman which, if accepted and reciprocated, will bring joy and well-being; reversed, an unworthy affection calculated to cause trouble.

Seven.—Trifling financial matters; reversed, money troubles.

Meaning of the Spades.

Ace.—Emotional enjoyment; reversed, news of a death, sorrow.

King.—A widower, an unscrupulous lawyer, impossible as a friend and dangerous as an enemy; reversed, the desire to work evil without the power.

Queen.—Widow, a very dark woman; reversed, an intriguing, spiteful woman.

Knave.—Legal or medical student, wanting in refinement of mind and manners; reversed, a treacherous character, fond of underhand measures.

Ten.—Grief, loss of freedom; reversed, passing trouble or illness.

Nine.—A bad omen, news of failure or death; reversed, loss of one near and dear by death.

Eight.—Coming illness; reversed, an engagement cancelled or a rejected proposal, dissipation.

Seven.—Everyday worries, or a resolve taken; reversed, silly stratagems in love-making.

CHAPTER IV. THE SIGNIFICATION OF QUARTETTES, TRIPLETS, AND PAIRS

COMBINATIONS OF COURT CARDS—
COMBINATIONS OF PLAIN CARDS—VARIOUS
CARDS READ TOGETHER—GENERAL
MEANING OF THE SEVERAL SUITS—SOME
LESSER POINTS TO NOTICE.

Combinations of Court Cards.

Four Aces.—When these fall together they imply danger, financial loss, separation from friends, love troubles, and, under some conditions, imprisonment. The evil is mitigated in proportion to the number of them that are reversed.

Three Aces.—Passing troubles, relieved by good news, faithlessness of a lover and consequent sorrow. If reversed, they mean foolish excess.

Two Aces.—These portend union; if hearts and clubs it will be for good, if diamonds and spades, for evil, probably the outcome of jealousy. If one or both be reversed, the object of the union will fail.

Four Kings.—Honours, preferment, good appointments. Reversed, the good things will be of less value, but will arrive earlier.

Three Kings.—Serious matters will be taken in hand with the best result, unless any of the three cards be reversed, when it will be doubtful.

Two Kings.—Co-operation in business, upright conduct and prudent enterprises to be crowned with success. Each one reversed represents an obstacle. All three reversed spell utter failure.

Four Queens.—A social gathering which may be spoilt by one or more being reversed.

Three Queens.—Friendly visits. Reversed, scandal, gossip, and possibly bodily danger to the inquirer.

Two Queens.—Petty confidences interchanged, secrets betrayed, a meeting between friends. When both are reversed there will be suffering for the inquirer resulting from his own acts. Only one reversed means rivalry.

Four Knaves.—Roistering and noisy conviviality. Any of them reversed lessens the evil.

Three Knaves.—Worries and vexations from acquaintances, slander calling the inquirer's honour in question. Reversed, it foretells a passage at arms with a social inferior.

Two Knaves.—Loss of goods, malicious schemes. If both are reversed the trouble is imminent; if one only, it is near.

Combinations of Plain Cards.

Four Tens.—Good fortune, wealth, success in whatever enterprise is in hand. The more there are reversed, the greater number of obstacles in the way.

Three Tens.—Ruin brought about by litigation. When reversed the evil is decreased.

Two Tens.—Unexpected luck, which may be connected with a change of occupation. If one be reversed it will come soon, within a few weeks possibly; if both are reversed, it is a long way off.

Four Nines.—Accomplishment of unexpected events. The number that are reversed stand for the time to elapse before the fulfilment of the surprise.

Three Nines.—Health, wealth, and happiness. Reversed, discussions and temporary financial difficulties caused by imprudence.

Two Nines.—Prosperity and contentment, possibly accompanied by business matter, testamentary documents, and possibly a change of residence. Reversed, small worries.

Four Eights.—Mingled success and failure attending a journey or the taking up of a new position. Reversed, undisturbed stability.

Three Eights.—Thoughts of love and marriage, new family ties, honourable intentions. Reversed, flirtation, dissipation and foolishness.

Two Eights.—Frivolous pleasures, passing love fancies, an unlooked-for development. Reversed, paying the price of folly.

Four Sevens.—Schemes and snares, intrigue prompted by evil passions, contention and opposition. Reversed, small scores off impotent enemies.

Three Sevens.—Sadness from loss of friends, ill-health, remorse. Reversed, slight ailments or unpleasant reaction after great pleasure.

Two Sevens.—Mutual love, an unexpected event Reversed, faithlessness, deceit or regret.

Various Cards Read Together.

The ten of diamonds next to the seven of spades means certain delay.

The ten of diamonds with the eight of clubs tells of a journey undertaken in the cause of love.

The nine of diamonds with the eight of hearts foretells for certain a journey.

The eight of diamonds with the eight of hearts means considerable undertakings; with the eight of spades there will be sickness; and with the eight of clubs there is deep and lasting love.

The seven of diamonds with the queen of diamonds tells of a very serious quarrel; with the queen of clubs we may look for uncertainty; with the queen of hearts there will be good news.

The ten of clubs followed by an ace means a large sum of money; should these two cards be followed by an eight and a king, an offer of marriage is to be expected.

When the nine, ace, and ten of diamonds fall together we may look for important news from a distance; and if a court card comes out after them a journey will become necessary.

The eight and seven of diamonds in conjunction imply the existence of gossip and chatter to be traced to the inquirer.

When the king, queen, knave, and ace of one colour appear in sequence it is a sign of marriage; should the queen of spades and the knave of hearts be near, it shows there are obstacles in the way; the proximity of the eight of spades bodes ill to the couple in question, but their happiness will be assured by the presence of the eight of hearts and the eight of clubs.

The ace of diamonds and the ten of hearts also foretell wedding bells.

The seven of spades, with either a court card or the two of its own suit, betrays the existence of a false friend.

The eight and five of spades coming together tell of jealousy that will find vent in malicious conduct.

A number of small spades in sequence are significant of financial loss, possibly amounting to ruin.

The king of hearts and the nine of hearts form a lucky combination for lovers.

The nine of clubs joined to the nine of hearts is indicative of affairs connected with a will likely to benefit the inquirer.

The queen of spades is the sign of widowhood, but if accompanied by the knave of her own suit she is symbolical of a woman who is hostile and dangerous to the inquirer.

General Meaning of the Several Suits.

Hearts, as might well be supposed, are specially connected with the work of Cupid and Hymen. The suit has also close reference to affairs of the home and to both the domestic and social sides of life.

Diamonds are mainly representative of financial matters. small and great, with a generally favourable signification.

Clubs are the happiest omens of all. They stand for worldly prosperity, a happy home life with intelligent pleasures and successful undertakings.

Spades, on the other hand, forebode evil. They speak of sickness, death, monetary losses and anxieties, separation from friends and dear ones, to say nothing of the minor worries of life. They are also representative of love, unaccompanied by reverence or respect, and appealing exclusively to the senses.

Some Lesser Points to Notice.

When a number of court cards fall together it is a sign of hospitality, festive social intercourse, and gaiety of all kinds. Married people who seek to read the cards must represent their own life partner by the king or queen of the suit they have chosen for themselves, regardless of anything else. For example, a very dark man, the king of spades, must consider his wife represented by the queen of spades, even though she may be as fair as a lily and not yet a widow.

Bachelors and spinsters may choose cards to personate their lovers and friends according to their colouring. Two red tens coming together foretell a wedding, and two red eights promise new garments to the inquirer.

A court card placed between two cards of the same grade—for instance, two nines, two sevens, &c., shows that the one represented by that card is threatened by the clutches of the law, and may be lodged at His Majesty's expense.

It is considered a good augury of success when, in dealing the cards out, those of lesser value than the knave are in the majority, especially if they are clubs.

Should a military man consult the cards he must always be represented by the king of diamonds.

It is always essential to cut cards with the left hand, there being a long-established idea that it is more intimately connected with the heart than the right. A round table is generally preferred by those who are in the habit of practising cartomancy. It is a matter of opinion as to whether the cards speak with the same clearness and accuracy when consulted by the inquirer without an intermediary. The services of an adept are generally supposed to be of great advantage, even when people have mastered the rudiments of cartomancy themselves.

Patience, the power of putting two and two together, a quick intuitive perception, and a touch of mysticism in the character, are all useful factors in the pursuit of this pastime.

CHAPTER V.

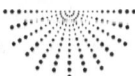

WHAT THE CARDS CAN TELL OF THE PAST, THE PRESENT, AND THE FUTURE A SIMPLE METHOD—WHAT THE CARDS SAY—THE PRESENT—THE FUTURE.

A Simple Method.

THERE is a very simple and generally accepted method of studying the past, the present, and the future in the light of cartomancy. The selected pack of thirty-two cards is required, and they must be shuffled and cut in the ordinary way. After the cut the packs must not be placed one upon the other until the top card of the lower one and the bottom card of the upper one have been placed aside to form the surprise. The remaining thirty cards are then to be dealt into three equal packs which, beginning at the left, represent respectively the Past, the Present, and the Future.

We will suppose that the knave of hearts, a pleasure-seeking young bachelor, is the inquirer.

The ten cards representing the Past are as follows:—

- The queen of clubs, reversed.
- The king of diamonds, reversed.
- The ten of clubs, reversed.
- The nine of diamonds.
- The eight of clubs.
- The ace of diamonds, reversed.
- The ace of hearts, reversed.
- The knave of spades, reversed.

- The queen of spades, reversed.
- The eight of diamonds.

There are three pairs among the ten. Two queens, both reversed, which remind the inquirer that he has had to suffer from the consequences of his own actions. The two aces, also both reversed, refer to some partnership into which he entered with good intentions but which was doomed to failure. The two eights speak of his frivolous pleasures and countless evanescent love affairs.

What the Cards Say.

We will now see what the cards have to say, taken in order. We begin with the queen of clubs, reversed, a dark woman tormented by jealousy, in which she was encouraged by the king of diamonds, reversed, who is a treacherous schemer, wishing no good to the inquirer. The ten of clubs tells of a sea voyage, and is followed by the nine of diamonds, showing that there were vexations and annoyances on that voyage. The eight of clubs speaks of the Inquirer's having possessed the affections of a dark woman, who would have contributed largely to his prosperity and happiness. The ace of diamonds, reversed, represents evil tidings that reached him in connection with the ace of hearts, reversed, which stands for a change of abode, and emanating from the knave of spades, reversed, a legal agent who was not to be trusted. There was also the queen of spades, a designing widow, with whom he had, the eight of diamonds, certain love passages.

The Present.

The ten cards in the centre pack are as follows:—

- Ace of spades, reversed.
- Seven of diamonds.
- Eight of hearts.
- Queen of hearts.
- Seven of hearts.
- Queen of diamonds, reversed.

- Nine of spades.
- King of hearts, reversed.
- Knave of hearts, reversed.
- Ten of diamonds.

In this pack we have only two pairs, two sevens speaking of mutual love; and two queens, one being reversed, which suggest rivalry.

Taken in order the pack reads thus:—

The ace of spades, reversed, speaks of sorrow in which he will be treated with a certain amount of heartless chaff and want of sympathy, as it is followed by the seven of diamonds. The eight of hearts tells us that he is entertaining thoughts of marriage, with the queen of hearts, a fair, lovable girl; but the seven of hearts shows that he is very contented with his present condition and in no hurry to change it. He is amusing himself with the queen of diamonds, reversed, who is a born flirt, but more spiteful than he suspects, and who is next to the worst card in the pack, the nine of spades, indicative of the harm she does to him, and the failure of his matrimonial plans. He is cut out by the king of hearts, who thus causes him a serious disappointment, and we see him, himself, reversed as the lover with a grievance; the last card is the ten of diamonds, so he has decided to ease his heartache by travelling.

The Future.

This pack contains the following cards:—

- The knave of diamonds, reversed.
- The seven of clubs.
- The eight of spades, reversed.
- The seven of spades, reversed.
- The ten of spades.
- The nine of hearts.
- The king of clubs.
- The ten of hearts.
- The king of spades.
- The ace of clubs, reversed.

The presence of four spades foretells that trouble awaits our bachelor. We again have a pair of sevens, but one is reversed, so he may expect deceit to be at work. The two tens promise him an unlooked-for stroke of tuck to be met with in a new walk in life, while the two kings speak of cooperation in business and of the success which will crown his upright and practical conduct. The wish card, the nine of hearts, and the ten of hearts in a great measure counteract the mischief represented by the spades.

The inquirer must beware of the knave of diamonds, reversed, who is a mischief maker, who will make use of the seven of clubs, trifling financial matters, either to break off an engagement or to cause an offer of marriage to be refused, as shown by the eight of spades, reversed. The chagrined lover will have recourse to silly stratagems in his love-making, the seven of spades, reversed, and this error will cause him grief, even to the shedding of tears, the ten of spades. The wish card, the nine of hearts, however, brings him better luck in his love affairs through the instrumentality of his trusty, generous friend, the king of clubs. His ill-fortune is further discounted by the next card, the ten of hearts, which promises him prosperity and success. He will find an enemy in the king of spades, a dark widower, who is a lawyer by profession, and none too scrupulous in his ways. He may expect a good deal of troublesome correspondence with this man, as shown by the last card, the ace of clubs, reversed.

The subject of this correspondence is possibly to be found in the surprise, which consists of the nine of clubs, reversed, meaning an unexpected acquisition of money under a will. He will do well to take heed when in the companionship of the knave of clubs, reversed, the second card of the surprise for he is a flatterer and a somewhat irresponsible character.

CHAPTER VI. YOUR FORTUNE IN TWENTY-ONE CARDS

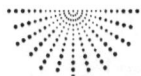

A REDUCED PACK—AN EXAMPLE—THE THREE PACKS—THE SURPRISE.

*T*HIS method requires a pack of thirty-two cards, although only twenty-one of them are actually used in the process. The whole pack must be well shuffled and cut with the left hand. The dealer then takes off the first eleven cards and throws them aside. From the twenty-one left in his hand he takes the uppermost card and places it apart for "the surprise" before dealing out the other twenty and placing them in order on the table before him. If the card representing the inquirer is not among them the whole process must be repeated from the beginning.

The signification of the cards must be read, taking care to notice any set of two, three, or four of a kind, as their collective meaning should be added to the individual explanation. After this has been done the twenty cards should be taken in order, starting from the left, and their meanings linked up together as a continuous message.

The cards must now be taken up again, shuffled, and cut as before. The dealer then makes them into three packs, having been careful to place the first card apart for "the surprise." Two of the packs will consist of seven cards, the third of only six. The inquirer is then asked to choose one of the packs, which must be exposed face upwards, moving from left to right, and these six or seven cards, as the case may be, should be read according to their significations. This operation is repeated three times, so that at the finish "the surprise" consists of three cards, which Are exposed and read last of all.

An Example.

The accompanying example will make the foregoing explanation more lucid and interesting.

We will take the knave of clubs as the representative of the inquirer, a dark, clever, well-intentioned young man. The twenty-one cards come out in the following order, beginning from the left:—

- The king of spades.
- Queen of hearts, reversed.
- Ace of hearts.
- Knave of clubs.
- Ace of spades, reversed.
- Ace of clubs.
- Knave of hearts.
- King of hearts.
- Queen of spades, reversed.
- Nine of hearts.
- Knave of diamonds.
- Ten of spades.
- Ace of diamonds, reversed.
- King of diamonds.
- Seven of diamonds.
- Eight of diamonds.
- Eight of spades, reversed.
- Seven of clubs, reversed.
- Nine of clubs, reversed.
- Nine of diamonds.

The surprise, placed apart.

Before taking the individual significance of each card we will look at some of the combinations. There are the four aces, telling of bad news, relating to trouble through the affections, but two being reversed mitigate the evil, and give a ray of hope to the inquirer. The three kings tell of an important undertaking which will be discussed and carried through successfully by the young man, who has excellent abilities.

The two queens, both reversed, warn the inquirer that he will suffer from the result of his own actions, more especially as the queen of spades in an inverted position represents a malicious and designing widow. It will be found as the process develops that she is very much to the fore with regard to the inquirer's affairs. The three knaves confirm the foregoing reading, for they betoken annoyances and worries from acquaintances, ending even in slander. The three nines, one of them reversed, speak of happiness and entire success in an undertaking, though the inversion shows that there will be a slight, passing difficulty to overcome. The two eights refer to flirtations on the part of the inquirer, and one being reversed warns him that he will have to pay for some of his fun. The two sevens tell of mutual love between the young man and the lady of his choice, but as the one is reversed there will be deceit at work to try and separate them.

Now let us see what the twenty cards have to say taken consecutively. We start off with the king of spades, a clever, ambitious, but unscrupulous man who has been instrumental in thwarting the love affairs of the fair, lovable, and tender-hearted woman, the queen of hearts, upon whom the inquirer has set his affections. The ace of hearts following her is the love letter she will receive from the inquirer, the knave of clubs; but he is next to the ace of spades, reversed, foretelling grief to him, which may affect his health, and the ace of clubs coming immediately after points to the cause being connected with money. The next three cards are court cards, and that means gaiety, in which the inquirer will be mixed up with a lively young bachelor—the knave of hearts—a fair, generous, but hot-tempered man—the king of diamonds—and the malicious, spiteful widow represented by the queen of spades, reversed. The inquirer will meet with pleasure, caused by success, the nine of hearts; but this is closely followed by the knave of diamonds, an unfaithful friend, who will try to bring disgrace, the ten of spades, upon his betters, and will write a letter containing unpleasant news—the ace of diamonds, reversed—which will concern or be prompted by the king of diamonds, a military man who has a grievance with regard to his love affairs and who is not above having recourse to scandal, the seven of diamonds, to avenge his wounded vanity. The next card is the eight of diamonds, the sign of some love-making, but our young people are not at the end of their troubles yet, for the eight of spades, reversed, tells us that his offer of marriage will be rejected. The seven of clubs is a card of caution, and implies danger from the opposite sea, so we gather that the spiteful widow has been at work, and is possibly to blame for his rejection; this idea is further strengthened by the nine of clubs, also reversed, coming immediately, which suggests letters that may have done the mischief. The nine of diamonds tells of the annoyance caused by these events, and their effect upon the affections of a dark person, the inquirer, who is a man well worth having.

The Three Packs.

In the first deal the inquirer chooses the middle pack, which contains the following cards: the knave of diamonds, the seven of diamonds, the ace of clubs, the queen of spades, reversed, the ace of spades, the ace of diamonds, the eight of diamonds.

We notice that three aces come out in this pack and show passing troubles in love affairs. The knave of diamonds, an unfaithful friend, is mixed up in scandal, the seven of diamonds, conveyed in a letter, the ace of clubs, written or instigated by the spiteful widow, the queen of spades. The ace of spades betokens sickness, but it is followed by the ace of diamonds, the wedding ring, and the pack closes with the eight of diamonds, telling of a happy marriage for the inquirer after all his worries.

In the second deal he again selects the middle pack, and we see the following: the queen of spades, reversed as usual, the nine of clubs, reversed, the seven of clubs, reversed, the nine of hearts, the seven of diamonds, the eight of clubs.

There are two nines, one reversed, speaking of small worries, and two sevens, one reversed, which show there is deceit at work. The pack reads thus: the queen of spades, the spiteful widow, who seems to be ubiquitous, is followed by the nine of clubs, representing the letter referred to above, and the seven of clubs standing next to it sounds a word of caution to the inquirer as to his lady friend, so-called; be will probably succeed in outwitting the widow, for the next card is the nine of hearts, implying joy and success in spite of scandal, the seven of diamonds with reference to his affections represented by the eight of clubs.

In the third deal the inquirer still is faithful to the middle

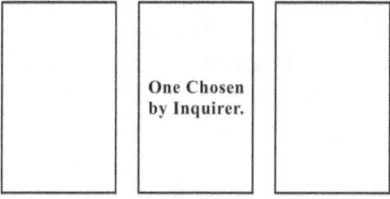

What the first selected pack contains—

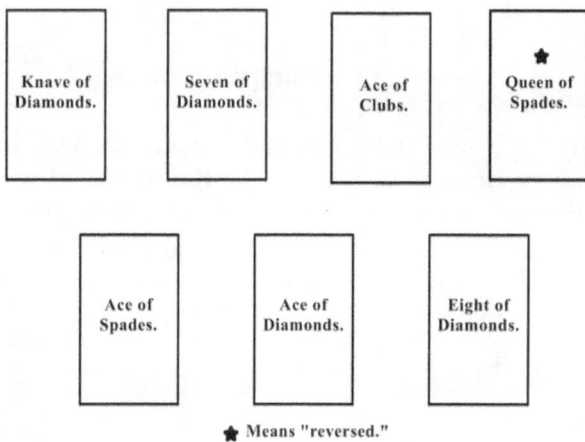

★ Means "reversed."

The three cards forming the Surprise—

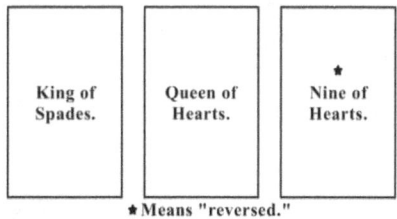

★ Means "reversed."

pack, and we find the following cards: the ace of diamonds, ten of spades, reversed, queen of spades, reversed, nine of diamonds, reversed, seven of clubs, reversed, ace of clubs, reversed.

The two aces, one of them reversed, tell of a union between two parties, but as the colours cross and one is reversed the result will not be known at. present. Here we get the wedding-ring, the ace of diamonds, followed by the ten of spades, reversed, which speaks of brief sorrow, occasioned doubtless by the spiteful widow, who again appears reversed, and intent upon mischief; next to her comes the nine of diamonds, reversed, signifying a love quarrel; the seven of clubs, reversed, gives a word of caution to the inquirer with regard to the opposite sex; the last card is the ace of clubs, reversed, which means joy soon followed by sorrow.

It is remarkable that the queen of spades comes out in each of the packs and is reversed every time.

The Surprise.

The surprise is now turned up and contains the king of spades, a dark, ambitious unscrupulous man who has interfered with the love affairs of the fair woman, the queen of hearts, to whom the inquirer has made an offer, so far without success; the third card is the nine of hearts, reversed, which tells that it will be but a passing cloud that will separate the lovers.

CHAPTER VII. COMBINATION OF SEVENS

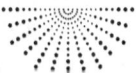

A METHOD WITH SELECTED CARDS—
GENERAL RULES—HOW TO PROCEED—
READING OF THE CARDS—SIGNIFICATION
OF CARDS—SOME COMBINATIONS—A
TYPICAL EXAMPLE—FURTHER INQUIRIES—
THE SEVEN PACKS.

A Method with Selected Cards.

THIS method is very simple, and as it takes but a short time, is more suitable when there are many fortunes to read. A little practice will soon enable a would-be cartomancer to construe the various combinations, as there are so few cards to remember.

It may be objected that meanings are now given different from those taught in the first method. This is certainly a fact, but it also an advantage; one method may suit one person's abilities and intuitiveness better than another, and so enable a more comprehensive reading to be given from the diminished pack than from the full Tarot pack.

General Rules.

Thirty-two cards only are selected from an ordinary pack of playing cards. In each suit the ace, king, queen, knave, ten, nine, eight, and seven are retained; all the others, those from two to six inclusively, are discarded.

The cards must be shuffled and cut into three sections by the inquirer, each cut being turned face upwards. The manipulator must carefully note the result of these cuts, as they give au indication of what is coming. Then the centre pack is to be takes first, the last neat, and the first last of all.

Holding this newly arranged pack in the left hand, draw off three cards, and facing them upwards, select the highest card of any suit that may appear. Retain this one and put the others aside for the next deal. Proceed in this way until you have finished the pack, then shuffle all the discard together, and repeat until you have any number over twenty-one on the table. If three cards of any suit should appear, or three cards of the same value, they are all to be taken.

It must not be forgotten that the cards are also selected from the "cuts," and should the lifting of one card reveal another of greater value of the same suit exposed, then that also is retained.

How to Proceed.

The first question to decide is which card will represent the inquirer. This is generally settled according to the complexion: diamonds for the very fair; hearts, those of medium colouring; clubs for brunettes with brown hair; and spades for those of dark complexion. This suit also represents elderly people. A king represents a man, and a queen a woman. This representative card is not to be drawn out; it is shuffled with the others, and taken when it is the highest of its suit. The only exception to this rule is, when there have been already twenty-one or more cards selected, then it must be taken from the remainder and placed last of all.

Reading of the Cards.

The reading in this method is from left to right, and the cards are to be placed in a semi-circle or horse-shoe, in the order they are drawn.

Court cards represent people, and the numbers relate to events. Generally diamonds relate to money and interest; hearts, to the affections; clubs, to business; spades, to the more serious affairs of life.

The signification of each card is given separately, as well as of some of the combinations, and an example of a fortune is worked out, the study of which will more easily enable a student to understand this method.

Signification of Cards.

HEARTS.

- *King.* — A man with brown hair and blue eyes.
- *Queen.* — A woman of similar complexion.
- *Knave.* — A friend with good intentions.
- *Ten.* — Marriage.
- *Nine.* — Wish.
- *Eight.* — Affection.
- *Seven.* — Friendship.
- *Ace.* — House.

DIAMONDS

- *King.* — A fair man.
- *Queen.* — A fair woman.
- *Knave.* — A friend.
- *Ten.* — Wealthy marriage.
- *Nine.* — Rise in social position.
- *Eight.* — Success with speculation.
- *Seven.* — A good income.
- *Ace.* — A wedding or present of jewellery.

CLUBS.

- *King.* — A man who is neither fair nor dark.
- *Queen.* — A woman in middle life.
- *Knave.* — A business friend.
- *Ten.* — Journey by water.
- *Nine.* — Successful business.
- *Eight.* — Pleasure in Society.
- *Seven.* — A business affair.
- *Ace.* — A letter, cheque, or legal document.

SPADES.

- *King.*—A dark man.
- *Queen.*—A dark woman (or widow).
- *Knave.*—Personal thoughts.
- *Ten.*—A journey by land.
- *Nine.*—Illness or sorrow.
- *Eight.*—A loss.
- *Seven.*—A disagreement
- *Ace (right way).*—Responsible position in the service of the Crown.
- *Ace (upside down).*—Sorrow or death.

Some of the Combinations.

Three kings—a new friend; two kings and a knave—meeting with an old friend; three knaves—legal business; three queens—a disagreement with women; three tens, very fortunate combination. If the ten of clubs and the ten of hearts appear with the ten of diamonds, it will easily be seen that a wealthy marriage will take place after a journey across the water.

Three nines—very speedy good news; three eights—a removal; three sevens—speedy news, but not altogether satisfactory; three aces—very good fortune; the ace of clubs and the ace of diamonds would signify an offer of marriage by letter.

The ace and nine of hearts mean that you will have the realisation of your heart's desire in your own house; the ace and nine of spades—that sorrow and death will come to your family; the king and queen of any suit, with the ten of hearts, Is a sign that you will hear of a marriage shortly.

A Typical Example.

Now we will proceed to read a fortune, and for the subject we will take the queen of hearts. The first shuffle and division of the pack into three reveals three hearts—king, knave, and seven—which indicates that the lady whom the queen represents has a firm man friend, who is neither fair nor dark. These three cards are taken and laid in order, beginning on the left hand.

Then the packs having been taken in order as described, and held in the left hand, the fortune-teller proceeds to draw off three cards, and make his selection according to the rule. The pack being finished, the process is repeated twice more.

In three deals the fortune of the queen of hearts revealed the following cards, and if a student will take a pack of cards and select the same, he can judge how the various combinations may be read.

King, knave, seven of hearts, ace of clubs, king of spades, queen of clubs, queen of diamonds, queen of spades, king of clubs, knave of diamonds, ace of hearts, knave of spades, king of diamonds, knave of clubs, queen of hearts, ace of diamonds, ten of hearts, eight of clubs, seven of spades, ace of spades, ten of clubs, ten of spades, ten of diamonds.

Now, from the queen of hearts we will proceed to count seven, taking into consideration the way the lady's face is turned. It is to the left, consequently the seventh card from her is the queen of spades, the seventh from which is the king of hearts, and the seventh again is the ten of hearts. I read this that the lady has some good friends; but that the woman whom the queen of spades represents will resent her marriage, but without effect. The next card is the knave of diamonds, followed by the seven of hearts and the seven of spades—a combination which represents some speedy news, not exactly to the advantage of the inquirer. The knave of spades, followed by the king and the ten of clubs, denotes that a dark man, who is separated from the queen of hearts, is constantly thinking of her and hoping for a speedy reunion.

The knave of clubs and the queen of diamonds come next. Knaves and women form a conjunction that never brings good luck; but in this case they are followed by the ten of diamonds, one of the most fortunate cards in the pack. The ace of diamonds and the king of clubs follow, which means an offer of marriage shortly. The queen of hearts is indeed a sad coquette, for there is no indication that she accepts this, as the knave of hearts, with the eight of clubs and the ace of hearts, are quickly on the scene. It appears that there is another wooer who comes to her home and is received with pleasure.

More serious affairs appear now; the ace of clubs, with the ace of spades and the king of diamonds, signify that the lady is likely to have some business with which a woman darker than herself is connected. This will lead to a considerable journey, which she will immediately take, as the card denoting this counts seven directly to her.

Now we will look at the cards as they lie on the table. For a reading taken at random they foretell a very good future. All the court cards and the aces and tens are out, with the seven of hearts and the eight of clubs, and all are cards of favourable import.

Three queens together generally betoken some mischief or scandal, but as they are guarded by kings it will probably not amount to much. The ace of diamonds and the ten of hearts placed so near the representative card would surely tell us of a forthcoming marriage, except that the queen has her face turned away from it. The three tens placed as they are tell of prosperity after journeys by land and water.

Now we will pair the cards and see if any more meaning can be extracted from them. On land and on the water this lady will meet a rich man who will entertain a strong affection for her. I must not omit to mention that the cards are paired from the extreme ends of the horse-shoe. Thus the king of hearts and the ten of diamonds, knave of hearts and ten of spades, &c. The business appears again, and a dark man seems to be in some perplexity. The three queens are not yet separated and are in closer connection with the inquirer than ever. Oh! there will be chatting over the tea-cups about a marriage. The fair damsel herself appears to be a little more inclined to matrimony, but the three knaves imply that she will have some difficulty in settling her affairs.

The two kings imply that she has some staunch friends, and that the result will be quite satisfactory. A general reading gives the impression that the queen of hearts is of a lovable disposition and fond of society, as so many court cards came out, and if the three queens meant a little gossip it was in a kindly spirit.

Further Inquiries.

There is another little ceremony to be gone through which will tell us if she is likely to have her "heart's desire" realised. The nine of hearts, which is the symbol of a wish, did not appear, so that she is apparently very cool and neutral. However, the other cards may tell us something.

The used cards are to be shuffled and cut once by the inquirer, and she may wish for anything she likes during the process. Then the cards are laid out one at a time in seven packs—six packs in a semicircle, and one in the centre—the cards of the last are to be turned face upwards, but none of the other cards are to be exposed until the end.

The Seven Packs.

The seven packs represent respectively—"yourself," "your house," "what you expect," "what you don't expect," "a great surprise," "what is sure to come true," and "the wish."

The cards, having been shuffled and cut once, are dealt out in the manner described, and these are the combinations we get:—

- *First Pack.*—Queen of spades, queen of hearts, ten of clubs, seven of hearts,
- *Second.*—Ace of spades, knave of clubs, ace of diamonds, and ten of spades.
- *Third.*—Knave of spades, king of diamonds, knave of hearts.
- *Fourth.*—Queen of clubs, seven of spades, king of spades.
- *Fifth.*—Ten of diamonds, eight of clubs, and queen of diamonds.
- *Sixth.*—King of hearts, ten of hearts, king of clubs. Wish.— Ace of hearts, knave of diamonds, ace of clubs.

The first pack represents to me the meeting of the inquirer with a dark or elderly woman, for whom she has a strong affection. Water is crossed before that meeting takes place.

The second pack reads as if a dark man would offer a ring or a present of jewellery, and also that he is meditating a journey by land. He is probably a professional man, or in the service of the Crown.

The third pack, with its combination of knaves and king, has reference to business transactions which will most probably be favourable to the interests of the queen.

The fourth pack presages some slight disappointment, illness, or unhappiness in connection with some friends.

The fifth pack tells us that same brilliant fortune is awaiting a fair friend that will lead to a higher social position.

The sixth pack tells us that, perhaps, our seemingly indifferent queen of hearts has a slight tenderness for some one. He is older than she is, and is only waiting for an opportunity to declare his affection. If the wish related to such a man as I have described, she may be certain of its fulfilment, even should there be a slight delay.

The seventh or wish pack is extremely good, and tells us that many affairs will be transacted by writing.

The future of the queen of hearts is fair and bright, her disposition is lovable, and she will bring happiness to other people.

This example is not made up of selected cards. They were shuffled, cut, and drawn in the ordinary way. I say this because so few cards of bad import have appeared, and it might be thought these were chosen in order to avoid prophesying disappointments.

In the foregoing example twenty-three cards were dealt out, but the number may vary. It must, however, be an uneven number. Sometimes only fifteen or seventeen cards are taken, and with the smaller quantity of selected cards there is an optional way of concluding operations. After having read the pairs, the cards are gathered up, shuffled, and cut into *three packs* instead of seven. These three are placed in a row, and a fourth card is put apart for *the surprise*. The inquirer is requested to choose one of the three packs, which represent respectively For *the house*, For *those who did not expect it*, and For *the inquirer*—the last being decided by the choice of the person in question.

When these three packs have been duly read, all the cards are again taken up except The Surprise (which is left face downwards on the table), and dealt out again, the same process being repeated three times until there are three cards set aside for the surprise. These are read last of all, and form the concluding message to the inquirer. Let's hope it may be a cheerful one!

CHAPTER VIII. ANOTHER METHOD

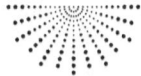

GENERAL OUTLINE—SIGNIFICATION OF CARDS—HOW TO CONSULT THE CARDS—AN ILLUSTRATION—ITS READING.

*H*ERE again the pack of thirty-two cards is used, the cards from two to six inclusively being discarded, as in "The Combination of Sevens."

General Outline.

The general meaning pertaining to each suit is as follows: The court cards bear the signification of people, and the king, queen, and knave in each suit suggest relationship. The kings indicate the profession followed.

Thus, the king of spades denotes a literary man, or one whose desires would lead him to the pulpit or the platform.

The king of hearts is the symbol of a wealthy man—one who deals with large sums of money—for instance, a banker, capitalist, or stockbroker.

The king of clubs indicates the mental side of business, and here we look for the lawyer or barrister.

The king of diamonds is a business man—one who will depend on both his brain and hands for work. Diamonds are eminently the practical suit, and must always be consulted with reference to the subject's condition in life. They signify the material side of life, and according to the needs, so this suit indicates success, or the absence of it—failure.

There is a very slight variation in the signification of the cards as given in the preceding method, but it is well to observe it carefully, as the mode of procedure is entirely different.

Signification of Cards.

HEARTS.

- *Ace.*—Quietness and domestic happiness.
- *Seven.*—Love.
- *Eight.*—A surprise.
- *Nine.*—A wish.
- *Ten.*—A wedding.

SPADES.

- *Ace.*—Service under the Crown.
- *Reverse ace.*—A death.
- *Seven.*—Unpleasant news.
- *Eight.*—Sorrow or vexation.
- *Nine.*—Quarrels.
- *Ten.*—A disappointment.

DIAMONDS.

- *Ace.*—A letter or ring.
- *Seven.*—A journey.
- *Eight.*—Society.
- *Nine.*—Illness, or sews of a birth.
- *Ten.*—Money, joy, success.

CLUBS.

- *Ace.*—A present.
- *Seven.*—Gain; good business.
- *Eight.*—Pleasure.
- *Nine.*—A proposal.
- *Ten.*—A journey by water.

How to Consult the Cards.

The inquirer is to shuffle the pack of cards and cut it into three. Take up the cards and let your subject draw any chance card that he pleases. Place this card on the table, and the suit from which it is drawn will determine the representative card, as it is an indication of the character of your subject.

A lady is represented by a queen, a man by a king, and the knave stands for the male relations or thoughts.

After the card is drawn, place the remainder on the table in four rows, beginning each row from left to right.

The cards that immediately surround the king or queen aid us in our judgment of the inquirer; and remember that the right hand card is the more important one.

An Illustration.

A practical illustration will exemplify my meaning, and again we will suppose a lady has cut the cards to have her fortune read.

The cards being shuffled and cut into three, the card was drawn, and as this proved to be a seven of clubs, so the queen represented the subject in this instance. When the cards were placed in order this is how they appeared.

First line.—Seven of clubs, eight of clubs, king of clubs, seven of hearts, king of diamonds, nine of diamonds, ten of diamonds, king of hearts.

Second line.—Seven of spades, nine of spades, knave of hearts, king of spades, eight of spades, queen of spades, ten of spades, ace of diamonds.

Third line.—Ace of spades, knave of clubs, queen of clubs, ten of hearts, ace of hearts, queen of diamonds, ace of clubs, nine of hearts.

Fourth line.—Knave of spades, seven of diamonds, eight of hearts, nine of clubs, eight of diamonds, knave of diamonds, queen of hearts, ten of clubs.

Its Reading.

Now we can proceed with the reading:—

As the suit of clubs is a pleasant one, we may conclude the lady is of a cheerful temperament. The seven itself signifies gain and prosperity, and the eight pleasure, which come to the inquirer through the king of clubs—typical of a solicitor. The seven of hearts indicates that a fair man is in love with the inquirer. The nine of diamonds, with the joyful ten beside it, seems to foretell a birth, and the king of hearts stands for a good friend. But the seven and nine of spades, in conjunction, inform us that some annoyance is coming which is possibly connected with the king of hearts.

The king of spades, accompanied by the eight of that suit, tells that this man is suffering considerable grief and vexation on account of the queen of clubs, suffering which will cause another woman to be jealous.

The queen and ten of spades, with the ace of spades, imply disagreeable tidings; but as the knave of clubs appears side by side with the queen of that suit (the inquirer), and they are followed by the ten of hearts, it will in no wise disturb the affection of either. The knave here may be taken to indicate the thoughts or intentions of the king. The ace of hearts seems to promise great tranquillity and happiness in the domestic life. A near relation, one deeply interested in the queen of clubs, is represented by the queen of diamonds. The ace of clubs shows that a letter is on its way.

The nine of hearts, the wish or betrothal card, follows, and from this I should infer that a proposal of marriage will come by letter, and one which will most probably be accepted. The knave of spades is followed by the seven of diamonds and the eight of hearts, which shows that the queen of clubs has been much loved by some one, and that an offer of marriage will have to be considered either directly before or immediately after a journey. The inquirer will have a great deal of pleasure on a journey. The queen of hearts and knave of diamonds indicate good friends who show her much kindness, and there will be welcome tidings for her across the water.

Now, count the rows, and should the betrothal card (the nine of hearts) appear in the third or fourth row, that number of years must elapse before becoming affianced.

Count the rows again until the one in which the ten of hearts (the marriage card) appears. In this example the betrothal and marriage card both appear in the third row, which indicates that the inquirer will be engaged in about three years, and marriage will take place soon after.

CHAPTER IX. A FRENCH METHOD

FRENCH SYSTEM—THE READING—AN EXAMPLE.

French System.

*T*AKE the pack of thirty-two cards, shuffle them thoroughly, then cut them in the usual way and deal them out in two packs of sixteen cards each. The inquirer must choose one of the packs and the first card is placed apart to supply the surprise. The remaining fifteen cards must then be turned face upwards, and placed in order, from left to right, before the dealer. It is essential that the card representing the inquirer should be found in the pack selected by him or her, otherwise it is useless to proceed; so the cards must be shuffled, cut, and dealt out over and over again, until the representative card is found in the right quarter.

The Reading.

The reading is conducted as follows. First, take any two, three, or four of a kind, kings, knaves, eights, or whatever may appear, and give their explanation as pairs, triplets, or quartettes; then start from the representative card, and count in sevens, moving from right to left; thirdly, pair the end cards together and consider their meaning. The next move is to shuffle the fifteen cards again, cut, and deal them out into three packs, each of which will naturally have five cards. The uppermost card of the three packs is removed, and placed with that which has been set apart for "The Surprise," and by this arrangement there will be four packs containing an equal number of cards.

The inquirer must then be asked to choose one of these packs for himself or herself, after which the four cards are exposed on the table from left to right, and their individual and collective meanings are read. The left hand pack will be for "The House," the third pack is "For Those Who do not Expect It," and the fourth supplies "The Surprise."

An Example.

Here is an example of the way in which the packs may turn out. We will suppose that the inquirer is represented by the queen of clubs. Her choice falls on the middle pack, which contains the following cards: the knave of clubs, the eight of diamonds, reversed,, the eight of hearts, and the queen of spades.

1. FOR THE INQUIRER.

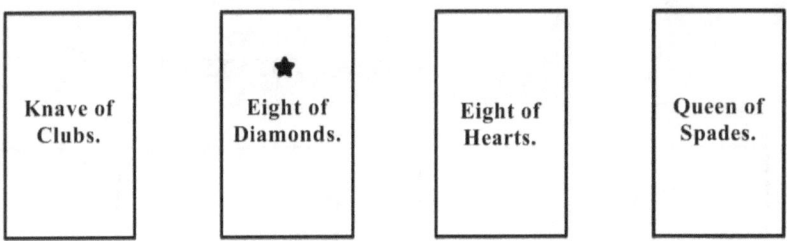

The reading will be thus, taking the cards in the above order;—The thoughts of the inquirer are running upon an unsuccessful love-affair, and, though moving in good society, she is exposed to the interference of a dark, malicious widow.

The next pack, standing for "The House," is made up of the knave of spades, the ace of spades, the king of spades, and the knave of hearts. We will take their signification as they stand. The three spades mean disappointment. The presence of two knaves together speaks of evil intentions.

The legal agent, knave of spades, is employed in some underhand business by his master, king of spades, the dishonest lawyer, who is an enemy to the inquirer just as he is that of her friend, the festive, thoughtless young bachelor, knave of hearts, who follows him.

2. THE HOUSE.

| Knave of Spades. | Ace of Spades. | King of Spades. | Knave of Hearts. |

The third pack is composed of the nine of clubs, reversed, the ace of clubs, the ten of spades, and the queen of hearts. We find short-lived joy and good news, followed by tears, for the fair, soft-hearted lady, who is susceptible to the attractions of the other sex.

3. FOR THOSE WHO DO NOT EXPECT.

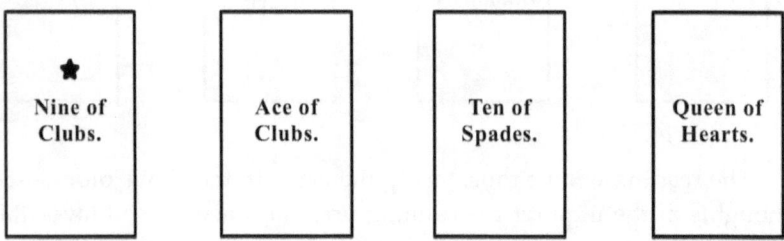

| Nine of Clubs. | Ace of Clubs. | Ten of Spades. | Queen of Hearts. |

"The Surprise" is very closely connected with the inquirer herself, for we find her included in the four cards. There are the ace of hearts, the queen of clubs, the nine of diamonds, and the seven of diamonds. From this we gather that there is a love letter for the inquirer, which, however, may be delayed by some cross accident, and she will thus be exposed to the foolish ridicule of tactless, unkindly persons. But she will get the letter all the same.

4. THE SURPRISE.

| Ace of Hearts. | Queen of Clubs. | Nine of Diamonds. | Seven of Diamonds. |

CHAPTER X. THE GRAND STAR

THE NUMBER OF CARDS MAY VARY—THE METHOD—THE READING IN PAIRS—DIAGRAM OF THE GRAND STAR—AN EXAMPLE.

The Number of Cards may Vary.

*T*HERE are various ways of telling fortunes with cards arranged in the form of a star, and whichever of these may be preferred, it will always be found necessary to use an uneven number of cards in addition to the one representing the inquirer. Some stars are done with thirteen cards, some with fifteen, and so on, but the real Grand Star must have twenty-one cards placed round the representative one.

The Method.

Suppose the inquirer be a fair man, the king of hearts would be the card selected to form the centre of the star. This representative card is placed face upwards on the table, and the remaining thirty-one cards of the pack (the twos, threes, fours, fives, and sixes having been previously removed) must then be shuffled, and cut with the left hand.

In the accompanying diagram the cards are numbered in the order that they are placed in upon the table, taking the representative as No. 1. The mode of withdrawing the cards from the pack is as follows: The first ten cards are thrown aside after the first cut, and the eleventh card is placed *below* No. 1; then cut out a second time, and place the *top* card of the pack on the table *above* No. 1; cut a third time, take the bottom card of the pack in the hand and place it to the left of No. s. The cards must be cut every time a card is to be withdrawn, and they are taken alternately from the top and bottom of the pack as above directed. Great care should be observed in the placing of the cards in due order, as any deviation will affect the reading at a subsequent stage of the process. The last card, No. 22, is placed across the foot of the representative.

The Reading in Pairs.

When the Grand Star has been thus formed, the cards must read in pairs, taking the outside circle in this order: 14 and 16, 21 and 19, 15 and 17, 20 and 18. Then take the inner circle, moving from left to right thus: 6 and 10, 9 and 12, 8 and 13, 7 and 11; the four centre points are paired thus: 4 and 2, 5 and 3; and the last card, No. 22, is taken separately. The significations are, of course, taken with regard to the relative positions of the cards, and their special reference to the central figure of the inquirer. This is a picturesque and simple way of consulting the cards, and will probably be a favourite with most people.

Diagram of the Grand Star.

The central card, No. 1, represents the inquirer, and each card is numbered in the order in which it is taken from the pack.

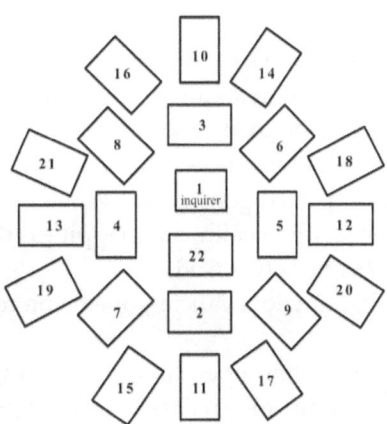

We will take the king of hearts as representative of the inquirer, and the twenty-one cards come out in the following order:—

- 1. King of hearts.
- 2. Ten of spades.
- 3. Ten of hearts.
- 4. Ace of hearts.
- 5. Nine of spades.
- 6. Ace of spades.
- 7. Nine of diamonds, reversed.
- 8. Queen of hearts.
- 9. Knave of diamonds.
- 10. Queen of spades.
- 11. Knave of clubs.
- 12. King of clubs.
- 13. Eight of clubs.
- 14. Queen of diamonds.
- 15. Nine of clubs, reversed.
- 16. King of spades.
- 17. Queen of clubs.
- 18. Eight of diamonds, reversed.
- 19. Ace of diamonds.
- 20. Knave of spades.
- 21. Knave of hearts.
- 22. Ace of clubs.

Before taking the above in pairs as directed, it will be well to glance at the groups contained in the star as it lies before us. We find:—

- *Four aces.*—Love troubles and hasty news for the inquirer.
- *Three kings.*—Success in an important undertaking.
- *Four queens.*—A good deal of social intercourse.
- *Four knaves.*—Somewhat noisy conviviality.
- *Two tens.*—Unexpected good luck.
- *Three nines.*—Health, wealth, and happiness discounted by imprudence as one is reversed.
- *Two eights.*—Passing love fancies, one being reversed.

The king of hearts, a fair, open-handed, good-natured man is the starting-point in reading the pairs which surround him. He is connected with (14) the queen of diamonds, a fair woman with a tendency to flirtation. She is amusing herself with (16) a very dark man, probably a lawyer, of an ambitious and not too scrupulous character, who does not wish well to the inquirer. The next pair (21) shows the knave of hearts, representing Cupid, or the thoughts of the one concerned, linked with (19) the ace of diamonds, a wedding ring. While this important item is occupying his thoughts he gives a small present (15), the nine of clubs, reversed, to (17) the queen of clubs, a charming dark lady, who is the real object of his affections. (20) The knave of spades, figuring a legal agent, or the wily lawyer's thoughts, makes mischief, and (18) the eight of diamonds, reversed, causes the inquirer's love-making to be unsuccessful. (6) The ace of spades warns the inquirer against false friends who will frustrate his matrimonial projects, and in (10) we find one of them, the queen of spades, a widow with possible designs upon him herself; (9) the knave of diamonds, reversed, shows the mischief-maker trying to breed strife with the inquirer's trusty friend (12), the king of clubs, and (8) the queen of hearts, a fair lovable woman possessing (13) eight of clubs, a dark person's affections; (7) the nine of diamonds, reversed, tells of a love quarrel, owing to (11) the knave of clubs, reversed, a harmless flirt The inquirer will get (4) the ace of hearts, a love letter, but his happiness will be succeeded by (2) the ten of spades, a card of bad import; (5) the nine of spades, tells of grief or sickness, possibly news of a death; but (3) the ten of hearts, counteracts the evil, and promises happiness to the inquirer, who shall triumph over the obstacles in his path, and find (22) joy in love and life.

CHAPTER XI. IMPORTANT QUESTIONS

HOW TO ANSWER THEM—SPECIMEN QUESTIONS—CUPID AND VENUS AT WORK.

How to Answer Them.

WHEN an answer to an important question is required, and the inquirer wishes to consult the cards on the subject, the following simple method may be adopted.

Let the question be asked by the inquirer, then let the dealer take the pack of thirty-two cards, which must be shuffled and cut in the usual manner. The dealer throws out the first eleven cards, which are useless, and proceeds to turn up the others upon the table. The answer is determined by the absence or presence of the special cards applying to each question among the exposed twenty-one.

Specimen Questions.

We will give some examples. Suppose the question to be:—

"*How far off is the wedding?*"

The needful cards in this case are the queen of spades, who should come out with or near the queen of hearts, and the ace of spades, which should accompany the eight of diamonds. These must be taken in conjunction with the other eights—each of which signifies a year; the four nines—each of which stands for a month; and the four sevens—each of which represents a week. Supposing the above-named cards—the two queens, the ace of spades, and the eight of diamonds—should not come out in due order, or be absent altogether, it may be feared that the date is postponed to vanishing point.

"Have I real cause for jealousy?"

If the seven of diamonds comes out in the first fifteen cards, the answer is "Yes." If the five of hearts and the seven of clubs appear instead among the first fifteen, it means "No."

"Shall we be parted?" or *"Shall I sustain the loss of my goods?"*

If the four nines are included in the twenty-one cards, the answer is "Yes." Should the four kings and the four queens come out, the meaning is "No, never! "

"Shall I succeed in my present or projected undertaking?"

To ensure a favourable answer the four aces and the nine of hearts must come out. Should the nine of spades appear just before the card representing the inquirer, it prognosticates failure, sure and certain.

"Will the change of residence or condition that I am considering be satisfactory?"

Should this question be asked by the master or mistress of a house, or an employer of labour, a favourable answer is secured by the presence of the four knaves, the eight and ten of diamonds, and the ten of clubs. In the event of the inquirer being an *employé*, or a paid worker of any grade, the twenty-one cards must include the ten and seven of diamonds, the eight of spades, and the four queens, to ensure a satisfactory reply. In both cases the nine of diamonds means hindrances and delay in attaining success.

"What fortune does the future hold for this child?"

The four aces foretell good luck and a suitable marriage. If the child in question be a girl, the four eights and the king of hearts should come out to secure peace and concord for her ie the home of her husband.

Cupid and Venus at Work.

Among the many ways in which cards can be used to provide entertainment, seasoned with a spice of the unexplainable, the following round game may be given a prominent place The ace of diamonds is the most valuable asset in winning tricks, as it takes all the other cards. The pack of fifty-two cards is used.

- The queen of hearts represents Venus.
- The knave of hearts stands for Cupid.
- The knave of diamonds, The knave of clubs, The knave of spades—all represent sweethearts.
- The ace of hearts—a new house.
- The ace of clubs—conquest.
- The two of diamonds—the ring and marriage.
- The twos of clubs, spades, and hearts—good luck.
- The threes—show surprise.
- The fours—that present conditions will remain unchanged.
- The fives—lovers' meetings.
- The sixes—pleasure.
- The sevens—disappointment.
- The eights—mirth.
- The nines—changes.
- The tens—marriage settlements.
- The queens represent women.
- The kings represent men.

Any number may take part in the game. The dealer Is chosen by lot, and when this has been settled, he or she proceeds to deal out the cards, leaving ten face downwards on the table. The stakes are agreed upon, and each player puts into the pool, the dealer being expected to pay double for the honour done to him by the fates.

The cards are then taken up, and each player looks at his own hand. The dealer calls for the queen of hearts, Venus, who ranks next to the ace of diamonds in value. Should any one have the ace of diamonds in his hand, he plays it straight out. Should the ace not be among those that have been dealt round, the queen of hearts is supreme, and the happy holder of Venus may look confidently forward to standing before the altar of Hymen during the current year. The ace of diamonds only counts as one card, but should any lucky player hold both Cupid and Venus in his hand he is entitled to clear the pool, and so end the game right off. In the event of the holder of these cards being married, their presence promises him some special stroke of good fortune.

When the matrimonial cards are out, or proved absent, the game is played on similar lines to whist, the same order of precedence being observed in taking tricks, and the larger the number secured the better the luck of the winner during the current year.

The nine of spades is the worst card in the pack, and the unfortunate holder has to pay for its presence in his hand by a treble stake to the pool. Should any player fail to win any tricks, he must pay in advance the stakes agreed upon for the next game.

Marriage by Lot.

For this appeal to the fates we require a pack of cards, a bag, and stakes either in money or counters. When the players have fixed upon their stakes and placed them in the pool, one of those playing must thoroughly shuffle the pack of cards and place them in the bag. The players then stand in a circle and draw three cards in turn from the bag as it is handed to each of them. Pairs of any kind win back the stakes paid by the holder, and promise good luck in the immediate future. The knave of hearts is proclaimed to represent Hymen. He wins double stakes, and is a happy augury that the holder will soon be united to the partner of his tit her choice. Should Venus, the queen of hearts, be found in the same hand, the owner takes the pool and wins the game. Fours and eights are losses and crosses, compelling a pre-arranged payment to the pool in addition to the usual stakes. A lady who draws three nines may resign herself to a life of single-blessedness, and the one who has three fives must prepare to cope with a bad husband.

Your Fate in Twenty Cards.

Only three or four girls are required to pursue this search for hidden knowledge. All the kings, queens, knaves, aces, and threes must be taken from the pack and dealt round to the players. Each one examines her hand for an answer to her inward questionings. The one who holds the most kings possesses the largest number of friends. The one with most queens has a proportionate number of enemies. Where kings and queens are united, there is the promise of speedy and happy marriage. Should a queen come out with knaves, we may be sure that intrigues are being woven round some unlucky person. Knaves by themselves represent lovers. Threes are evil omens betokening great sorrow. A knave with four threes means that the fair holder will not enter the holy estate. A king with four threes encourages her to hope, for she has a good chance of matrimony. A queen with four threes is the worst combination a girl can draw, for it speaks of sorrow deepened by disgrace. Mixed hands have no special significance, nor is there any great meaning attached to the four aces. Where only two or three of one kind of card fall together, the meaning ascribed to the four collectively is lessened in proportion to the number held.

Hearts are Trumps.

This game might by some be called an apology for whist. Four players, or three and a dummy, are necessary, and the whole pack is dealt out in the usual way. Hearts are trumps in every deal, and carry everything before them. The highest card is the queen, who is the goddess of love, and takes precedence of the ace, which only counts as one. The person on the left hand of the dealer leads trumps, and the stronger the hand the better the chances for love and marriage. The one who wins the largest number of tricks has, or will have, the most lovers. The presence of the king and queen of trumps in one hand is the sign of a speedy union of hearts, and of the approaching sound of wedding bells. A sorry fate awaits the luckless maid or youth who is without a heart—in the hand—for Cupid and Hymen have turned their faces away, and no luck will come of a love affair in that quarter. Where only one or two small trumps can be produced, the holder will have to wait long for wedded bliss. Each one plays quite independently of the others, and the one who undertakes dummy must not connect its cards in nay way with those he holds himself.

Another Lottery.

Put a well-shuffled pack of cards into a bag deep enough to prevent the contents from being seen. An uneven number of girls must then form a ring round the one holding the bag, and each must draw a card. The cards thus drawn must then all be exposed, as they have to be compared. The lucky lady who draws the highest card will be the first to be led to the altar. She who draws the lowest will have to emulate Mariana of the Moated Grange, and resign herself to the fact that "he cometh not" for many weary days to follow. Any one drawing the ace of spades may cheerfully prepare for the pleasures of a bachelor life. The nine of hearts is the presage of serious trouble, coming to the holder through loving "not wisely but too well"

CHAPTER XII. HOW THEY TELL FORTUNES IN ITALY

ITALIAN METHOD—AN EXAMPLE—NOTICE THE GROUPS—HOW THE PAIRS WORK OUT—THE FIVE PACKS.

Italian Method.

ONLY thirty-two cards are used for the Italian method of fortune-telling, all the numbers under seven, except the ace, being taken out of each suit. This reduced pack—containing the ace, king, queen, knave, ten, nine, eight, and seven of the four suits—must be carefully shuffled and cut, with the left hand of course, by the inquirer. The one who is going to act as interpreter then takes the pack, and turns them up three at a time. Should three cards of one suit be turned up at once, they are all laid upon the table, face upwards; if only two of a suit come out together, the higher card is selected; if all three belong to different suits, they are all rejected.

When the pack has been dealt out in this manner the cards that have not been chosen are taken up, shuffled, and cut a second time. The deal by threes is then repeated until there are fifteen cards upon the table. They must be placed in line, from left to right, as they appear.

It is absolutely necessary that the card representing the inquirer should be among those on the table. Some authorities maintain, however, that in the event of its not coming out during the deals, the whole process must be repeated until it makes its appearance. Others again take the card out, and place it on the table when fourteen others have been selected.

The next step is to count five cards from the representative one and to continue counting in fifths from each fifth card until all have been included, or the counting has come back to the representative. The signification of every card is read as it is reached, due notice being taken as to whether it is reversed or not, and the surrounding circumstances must also be balanced by the interpreter.

When this reading is complete the fifteen cards must be paired, one from each end of the line being taken and read together, while the remaining odd one must be dealt with separately.

The third process is to shuffle and cut the fifteen cards, and deal them out into five small packs: one for *the lady herself;* one for *the house;* one for *those who do not expect it;* one for *those who do expect it;* one for *the surprise;* and one, which is not to be covered, for *consolation.* When the fifteen cards have been dealt out, it will be seen that four of the packs contain three cards, and the fifth only two. These must all be turned face upwards and read in separate packs, but with the connecting idea that they all refer to the fortune of the inquirer.

An Example.

Let us imagine that a very fair lady, represented by the queen of diamonds, is seeking to read her fortune.

The fifteen cards come out in the following order:—

The queen of diamonds; nine of diamonds, reversed; queen of hearts; king of spades; ten of diamonds; seven of diamonds, reversed; knave of hearts, reversed; ten of hearts; knave of diamonds; ace of diamonds, reversed; knave of spades; nine of spades; king of clubs; ten of spades, reversed; ace of hearts.

We begin to count from the queen of diamonds, the representative card, and find the nine of diamonds to be the fifth from it. By this first count we see from the nine being reversed that there is a love quarrel troubling the inquirer. Starting again from the nine we come to the queen of hearts, a mild, good-natured, but not very wise woman, who is probably the tool of the next fifth card, the king of spades, a crafty, ambitious man, and an enemy to the queen of diamonds.

Our next count is to the ten of diamonds, which speaks of a journey for the inquirer. Passing on to the seven of diamonds, reversed, we get hold of a foolish scandal connected with, if not entirely caused by, the next count, which is the knave of hearts, reversed, and stands for a military man who is very discontented with the treatment he has received at the hands of the fair inquirer. She will, however, triumph over this foolish annoyance, for the ten of hearts comes next in order, and counteracts the harm involved by the other cards.

Our gentle lady has, unfortunately, an unfaithful friend in the knave of diamonds; and he is followed by the ace of diamonds, reversed, which portends a letter on the way containing bad news. The writer of this is a dark young man of no social position, and he probably is the servant of one who is dear to the queen of diamonds. The bad news is found in the next count, the nine of spades, which tells of sickness affecting the king of clubs, the warm-hearted, chivalrous man who occupies the first place in the inquirer's affections. The last count but one brings us to the ten of spades, reversed, by which we know that the lady's sorrow will be but brief; and it is followed by the ace of hearts, a love letter containing the good news of her lover's recovery.

Notice the Groups.

Before proceeding to pair the cards, we may as well note the groups as they have come out in the fifteen. The six diamonds point to there being plenty of money; the two tens tell of a change of residence, either brought about by marriage, or by the journey read in the ten of diamonds; the presence of three knaves betokens false friends, though as one is reversed, their power of doing harm is lessened; two queens indicate gossip and the revealing of secrets; the two aces imply an attempted plot, but it is frustrated by the one being reversed; the two nines also point to riches.

How the Pairs Work Out.

The two end cards of the fifteen are taken up together, so that the pairs shall work out thus:—The queen of diamonds and the nine of spades, implying that sickness and trouble will affect the inquirer; the ten of diamonds pairs with the ten of hearts, and they signify a wedding; the knaves of diamonds and spades coming together show evil intentions towards the inquirer; the king of clubs and the ace of hearts tell of the lover and the love letter; the inverted nine of diamonds pairing with the knave of spades, tells of a love quarrel, in which a dark young man, wanting in refinement, is concerned; the reversed seven of diamonds pairs with the knave of hearts, also inverted, and tells of a foolish scandal instigated by the ungallant soldier who is suffering from wounded vanity; the inverted ace of diamonds comes out with the queen of hearts, telling of a letter containing unpleasant news from a fair, good-natured woman; while the remaining card, the ten of spades, being inverted, speaks of brief sorrow for the inquirer.

The Five Packs.

Our next step is to deal out the five packs as already directed. The first one—for *the lady herself*—contains three cards, two of which are bad, but their harm is largely discounted by the ten of hearts. In the nine of spades we read of the trouble caused by her lover's illness; the ten of spades betokens the tears she will shed while the beloved life is in danger; the ten of hearts speaks of happiness triumphing over sorrow.

The second pack—for *the house*—contains a flush of diamonds, the ten, the ace, and the knave. There is plenty of money in the house: the ten speaks of a journey, possibly resulting in a change of residence; the ace, being reversed, tells of a letter on the way containing unpleasant news (probably connected with the removal), from the knave, who is a faithless friend, and is to blame for the annoyance.

The third pack—for *those who do not expect*—consists of three court cards, which taken together foretell gaiety of some sort. We find the inquirer, personated by the queen of diamonds, in the society of the knaves of spades and hearts, the latter reversed, and consequently we know that she will be troubled by some unfriendly schemes, in which the dark, undesirable young man and the disappointed officer will be concerned. The inversion of the one knave counteracts the intended harm.

The fourth pack—for *those who do expect*—contains the queen of hearts, the king of spades, and the seven of diamonds, inverted. These indicate that the fair woman of gentle and affectionate nature will be exposed to scandal, seven of diamonds reversed; through the agency of the king of spades, an ambitious untrustworthy lawyer who is her enemy.

The fifth pack, consisting of only two cards (the ace of hearts and the nine of diamonds), is for *the surprise,* and we learn that a love letter, the ace, will be delayed, the nine; but the consolation card is the king of clubs, the dark, warm-hearted man, who will come in person to his lady-love.

The above example has been taken in the plainest, most straightforward manner with just the most apparent reading of the cards given as an illustration of the method. Those who spend time and thought on the subject will soon get to see more of the "true inwardness" of the cards with respect to their relative positions, and their influence one upon another. Various experiments with this plan of fortune-telling will give rise to curious combinations, and perhaps startling developments, as the one acting for the inquirer gains in knowledge and confidence.

CHAPTER XIII. THE MASTER METHOD

KNOWLEDGE IS POWER—FOUR TWOS ADDED TO THE USUAL PACK—THE THIRTY-SIX SQUARES AND THEIR SIGNIFICANCE—TENDENCIES OF THE SUITS.

Knowledge is Power.

WE have here a detailed and exhaustive method by which the cards can be read. The beginner may feel somewhat alarmed at the mass of explanatory matter there is for him to study, but when once the information has been acquired, the would-be cartomancer will find he possesses a sense of power and comprehension, that will give both confidence and dexterity to his attempts to unravel the thread of destiny.

Four Twos Added to the Usual Pack.

The selected pack of thirty-two cards, which have been mentioned in connection with several of the preceding methods, are in this case augmented by the addition of the four twos, one of which is sometimes taken as the representative of the inquirer. There is no hard and fast rule about this, however, and another card may be taken if preferred. The accompanying table shows that not only has each card its own signification, but that every position upon the table within the cube in which the cards are arranged has its own meaning. These must be carefully studied, first separately and then together. It would be a help to the beginner to make a separate chart for his own use, and to have it at hand when laying the cards according to this system.

THE MASTER METHOD.

TABLE OF THE POSITIONS AND THEIR SEVERAL MEANINGS.

No. 1. Project in hand.	No. 2. Satisfaction.	No. 3. Success.	No. 4. Hope.	No. 5. Chance. Luck.	No. 6. Wishes. Desire.
No. 7. Injustice	No. 8. Ingratitude.	No. 9. Association.	No. 10. Loss.	No. 11. Trouble.	No. 12. State or Condition.
No. 13. Joy.	No. 14. Love.	No. 15. Prosperity.	No. 16. Marriage.	No. 17. Sorrow. Affliction.	No. 18. Pleasure. Enjoyment.
No. 19. Inheritance. Property.	No. 20. Fraud. Deceit.	No. 21. Rivals.	No. 22. A Present. Gift.	No. 23. Lover.	No. 24. Advancement. A Rise in the world.
No. 25. Kindness. A Good Turn.	No. 26. Undertaking. Enterprise.	No. 27. Changes.	No. 28. The End (of Life).	No. 29. Rewards.	No. 30. Misfortune. Disgrace.
No. 31. Happiness.	No. 32. Money. Fortune.	No. 33. Indifference.	No. 34. Favour.	No. 35. Ambition.	No. 36. Ill-health. Sickness.

The thirty-six cards must be shuffled and cut in the usual way, and then placed upon the table in six rows of six cards each, starting from the left-hand corner where square No. 1 is marked on the chart. The position of the inquirer must be carefully noted, and then all the cards in his immediate neighbourhood must be read in all their bearing, individually, and with regard to their position, and their influence upon the representative card.

The Thirty-Six Squares and their Significance.

We will take the meanings of the thirty-six squares in connection with the several cards that may cover them.

No. 1. THE PROJECT IN HAND.

- When covered by a heart, the inquirer may hope that the project will be successfully carried out.
- When covered by a club, kind and trusty friends will help forward the project.
- When covered by a diamond, there are serious business complications in the way of the project's accomplishment.
- When covered by a spade, the inquirer will have his trust abused and those in whom he has confided will play him false, to the detriment of the project in hand.

No. 2. SATISFACTION.

- When covered by a heart, the inquirer may look for the realisation of his brightest hopes and his dearest wishes.
- When covered by a club, satisfaction will be derived by the help of true friends, who will do all in their power to promote the inquirer's happiness.
- When covered by a diamond, there will be jealousy at work to mar the inquirer's satisfaction.
- When covered by a spade, the hope of success will be well-nigh shattered by deceit and double-dealing.

No. 3. SUCCESS.

- When covered by a heart, the inquirer may hope for complete success.
- When covered by a club, any success will be due to the help of friends.
- When covered by a diamond, the success will be but incomplete.
- When covered by a spade, all chance of success will be eventually destroyed by underhand means.

No. 4. HOPE.

- When covered by a heart, the inquirer may look for the fulfilment of his dearest hopes.
- Covered by a club, hopes will be realised through the agency

of helpful friends, or be due to the obstinate determination of the inquirer.
- Covered by a diamond, it shows that the hopes are groundless and impossible of realisation.
- Covered by a spade, wild hopes are indicated, tending to mania, and provocative of grave trouble, or even tragedy.

No. 5. CHANCE—LUCK.

- Covered by a heart, good luck will attend the hopes and plans of the inquirer.
- Covered by a club, means moderately good luck, especially due to the kindly offices of friends.
- Covered by a diamond, does not promise much luck to the inquirer; rather an evil than a good influence.
- Covered by a spade, bad luck, robbery, financial ruin, disaster, and possibly death.

No. 6. WISHES—DESIRE.

- Covered by a heart and surrounded by good cards, it promises the immediate fulfilment of the inquirer's highest desires.
- Covered by a club, a partial gratification of the inquirer's wishes may be expected.
- Covered by a diamond, the earnest efforts of both the inquirer and his friends will only be crowned with imperfect success.
- Covered by a spade, disappointment and non-fulfilment of desires.

No. 7. INJUSTICE.

- Covered by a heart, any injustice done to the inquirer will be rectified and withdrawn, so that the passing cloud will turn to his ultimate advantage.
- Covered by a club, the wrong already done will require long and courageous efforts to efface its effects, and the inquirer will need the support of his best friends.
- Covered by a diamond, the harm done will not be entirely

remedied, but the inquirer's good name will be re-established.
- Covered by a spade, injustice will bring about sore trouble and serious misfortunes.

No. 8. INGRATITUDE.

- The four suits have exactly the same influence upon the situation in this number as in the preceding one.

No. 9. ASSOCIATION.

- Covered by a heart, the partnership will be successful and have the best results.
- Covered by a club, good results of co-operation or partnership will be effected through the agency of true friends.
- Covered by a diamond, the inquirer will need to use all possible caution and diplomacy, and even then the results will be but unsatisfying.
- Covered by a spade, the connection will not benefit the inquirer, in fact he may suffer terribly from it, but his friends will profit thereby.

No. 10. LOSS.

- Covered by a heart, shows loss of a benefactor, which will be a great grief to the inquirer.
- Covered by a club, the loss of dear friends and the failure of cherished hopes.
- Covered by a diamond, loss of money, goods, property, and personal effects.
- Covered by a spade, the best interests of the inquirer will be seriously compromised, and he will have to renounce them.

No. 11. TROUBLE.

- Covered by a heart, very great trouble caused by near relations, or born of love for another.
- Covered by a club, trouble with friends.

- Covered by a diamond, money troubles.
- Covered by a spade, trouble arising from jealousy.

No. 12. STATE OR CONDITION.

- Covered by a heart, the conditions of life are steadily improving.
- Covered by a club, the improvement will be slower and more uncertain; hard work and good friends are essential to ensure advancement.
- Covered by a diamond, the inquirer will only attain to a satisfactory position in life after he has overcome numerous and powerful enemies. He will never get very far however.
- Covered by a spade, the inquirer's circumstances are bound to go from bad to worse, in spite of all he may do.

No. 13. JOY—DELIGHT.

- Covered by a heart, deep, unruffled delight, joy of a pure and disinterested nature.
- Covered by a club, joy from material causes, better luck or greater prosperity.
- Covered by a diamond, joy springing from success in profession or business, gained in spite of jealous opposition.
- Covered by a spade, joy from having been able to render a service to a superior, who will not forget it.

No. 14. LOVE.

- Covered by a heart, the inquirer will be blessed and happy in his love.
- Covered by a club, he may rely absolutely upon the fidelity of his beloved.
- Covered by a diamond, love will be troubled by jealousy.
- Covered by a spade, love will be slighted and betrayed.

No. 15. PROSPERITY.

- Covered by a heart, the inquirer will enjoy complete and well-merited prosperity.
- Covered by a club, betokens moderate prosperity, due to hard work and the kindly offices of friends.
- Covered by a diamond, prosperity will be damaged by the jealousy of others.
- Covered by a spade, serious misfortunes will arise in business, brought about by the malice and fraud of other people.

No. 16. MARRIAGE.

- Covered by a heart, the inquirer may look forward to a happy and well-assorted marriage.
- Covered by a club, foretells a marriage prompted by practical or financial considerations alone.
- Covered by a diamond, the married life will be troubled by the jealousy of one or both partners.
- Covered by a spade, inquirer will lose the chance of a wealthy marriage, through the deceit and jealousy of his enemies.

No. 17. SORROW—AFFLICTION.

- Covered by a heart, the inquirer will pass through a love trouble, but it will only be of short duration.
- Covered by a club, trouble will arise from a quarrel with a dear friend, but it will end in complete reconciliation.
- Covered by a diamond, there will be sorrow caused by jealousy.
- Covered by a spade, bad faith and underhand dealings will bring affliction upon the inquirer.

No. 18. PLEASURE—ENJOYMENT.

- Covered by a heart, the inquirer will enjoy the bliss of mutual love, undimmed by even passing clouds.

- Covered by a club, there will be love of a more imperfect and superficial character.
- Covered by a diamond, love will be tormented and distracted by jealousy.
- Covered by a spade, love will be unreal and evanescent, unable to bear the test of time, or to survive the first disagreement.

No. 19. INHERITED MONEY OR PROPERTY.

- Covered by a heart, the inquirer will come into a large inheritance, to which he has a legitimate and undisputed right.
- Covered by a club, a friend will bequeath a portion of his property or money to the inquirer.
- Covered by a diamond, the inquirer will lose part of his rights, owing to the jealousy of another person.
- Covered by a spade, an entire estate will be stolen from the inquirer by intriguing rivals.

No. 20. FRAUD—DECEIT.

- Covered by a heart, the deceiver will be caught in the trap he has laid for the inquirer.
- Covered by a club, by the aid of true friends the inquirer will escape from the effects of an act of treachery.
- Covered by a diamond, the inquirer will have to suffer great pain from the consequences of deceit, but it will only be a passing trouble.
- Covered by a spade, deceit and underhand dealings will culminate in calumny which will cost the inquirer many friends, and have serious consequences for him.

No. 21. RIVALS.

- Covered by a heart, the inquirer will obtain his desire in spite of powerful or puny rivals.
- Covered by a club, rivals will be overcome with difficulty, and with the help of generous friends.
- Covered by a diamond, a rival will so far outwit the inquirer

as to obtain some of the advantage, wealth, or favour for which he is striving.
- Covered by a spade, the rival will triumph over the inquirer, robbing him, and plunging him into disgrace both with his benefactors and with members of his own immediate circle.

No. 22. A PRESENT OR GIFT.

- Covered by a heart, the inquirer will have a very handsome and unexpected present.
- Covered by a club, the inquirer will receive a gift that is bestowed upon him from motives of self-interest, or in a spirit of vulgar display.
- Covered by a diamond, points to a gift intended to act as a bribe.
- Covered by a spade, indicates a present which is given to further the deceitful ends of the donor.

No. 23. LOVER.

- Covered by a heart, the lover or the lady, as the case may be, will be both fond and faithful in life and death.
- Covered by a club, the beloved will be faithful, but somewhat faulty in other respects.
- Covered by a diamond, the inquirer may be prepared to find the beloved both jealous and disposed to sulk.
- Covered by a spade, the beloved will prove faithless, selfish, and vindictive.

No. 24. ADVANCEMENT.

- Covered by a heart, the inquirer will soon see a rapid improvement in his worldly position, and it will exceed his wildest hopes.
- Covered by a club, there will be a moderate and satisfying advance in the inquirer's circumstances, which will be the result of his own hard work, aided by the sympathy and help of his friends. He will be contented and happy.
- Covered by a diamond, advancement will only be obtained

after a hard struggle against difficulties, caused by the jealous ill-will of others.
- Covered by a spade, the underhand dealings of his enemies will destroy all hope of a rise in the world.

No. 25. KINDNESS—A GOOD TURN.

- Covered by a heart, the inquirer will receive a kindness which far exceeds both his expectations and his deserts.
- Covered by a club, this good turn will be well deserved, but only obtained by the help of disinterested friends.
- Covered by a diamond, the inquirer will only obtain a modicum of kindness, and that after he has surmounted serious obstacles built up by the jealousy of his enemies.
- Covered by a spade, the inquirer will not benefit by the good turn which he well deserves, but he will have to see it diverted from him by double-dealing.

No. 26. UNDERTAKING—ENTERPRISE.

- Covered by a heart, whatever undertaking the inquirer has in hand will meet with signal success.
- Covered by a club, the enterprise will be a financial success, owing to the help of friends.
- Covered by a diamond, the success of the undertaking will be hindered and decreased by the jealousy and self-seeking of some people concerned in it.
- Covered by a spade, the inquirer must prepare for failure in his enterprise, owing to the malicious intrigues of his rivals.

No. 27. CHANGES.

- Covered by a heart, the change contemplated by the inquirer is a good one.
- Covered by a club, a change for the better will take place in the inquirer's circumstances, owing to the good offices of friends.
- Covered by a diamond, the inquirer will make an earnest attempt to change his position in life, but his efforts will be fruitless.

- Covered by a spade, a change, very much for the worse, is to be apprehended. It will be brought about by the malice and double-dealing of those who seek to harm him.

No. 28. THE END (OF LIFE).

- Covered by a heart, by the death of a relation or friend the inquirer will come into a considerable fortune.
- Covered by a club, a handsome legacy from a friend may be expected by the inquirer.
- Covered by a diamond, one who wishes ill to the inquires will depart this life.
- Covered by a spade, this portends the untimely death of the inquirer's greatest enemy.

No. 29. REWARD.

- Covered by a heart, the inquirer will be rewarded out of all proportion to his efforts.
- Covered by a club, a due and fitting reward will be meted out to industry and perseverance.
- Covered by a diamond, a well-merited reward will be hindered and reduced, by the unscrupulous action of others.
- Covered by a spade, the inquirer will be done out of his just reward, by the double-dealing and dishonesty of certain people.

No. 30. DISGRACE-MISFORTUNE.

- Covered by a heart, misfortune will come to the inquirer, but it will not do him any permanent harm.
- Covered by a club, the inquirer will suffer through the disgrace of a friend.
- Covered by a diamond, misfortune will be brought about by jealousy, and will indirectly affect the inquirer.
- Covered by a spade, dishonesty and double-dealing will cause disgrace, from which the inquirer will suffer long and acutely.

No. 31. HAPPINESS.

- Covered by a heart, the inquirer will experience unexpected happiness which will be both deep and lasting.
- Covered by a club, a stroke of luck will come to the inquirer, through the good offices of friends.
- Covered by a diamond, the jealousy and ambition of false friends will result in good fortune to the inquirer.
- Covered by a spade, the life of the inquirer will be in danger from the malice of his enemies. Their murderous schemes will be happily defeated by the vigilance of his friends.

No. 32. MONEY—FORTUNE.

- Covered by a heart, the inquirer will rapidly acquire a large fortune, by making a hit in his profession, or by a lucky speculation.
- Covered by a club, by hard work and sustained effort the inquirer will secure a competence, and will receive both help and encouragement from his friends.
- Covered by a diamond, through misplaced confidence in unworthy friends the inquirer will see his fortune pass into dishonest hands.
- Covered by a spade, not only will the inquirer be tricked out of his money by dishonest acquaintances, but he will have to suffer for their misdeeds in his business or profession.

No. 33. INDIFFERENCE.

- Covered by a heart, thanks to his indifference and want of heart the inquirer will lead an unruffled, if somewhat joyless, life.
- Covered by a club, lack of interest and energy will allow the inquirer to let slip things that would give him pleasure.
- Covered by a diamond, the inquirer will forfeit the love and regard of valuable friends owing to indifference and utter unresponsiveness.
- Covered by a spade, as a result of culpable indifference the inquirer will be robbed and impoverished.

No. 34. FAVOUR.

- Covered by a heart, the inquirer will enjoy all that love can bestow upon the beloved.
- Covered by a club, the inquirer will honestly seek and acquire the favour of influential persons.
- Covered by a diamond, the favour of the great will be long and earnestly sought by the inquirer, who will not succeed single-handed.
- Covered by a spade, no effort of any kind will admit the inquirer to the favour to which he aspires.

No. 35. AMBITION.

- Covered by a heart, the inquirer will shortly arrive at the highest point of his ambition.
- Covered by a club, the moderate ambition of the inquirer will be realised.
- Covered by a diamond, the lawful ambitions of the inquirer will be partially frustrated, by the ill-will and jealousy of certain acquaintances.
- Covered by a spade, the principal ambition of the inquirer will be defeated by underhand transactions, and he will even suffer from the consequences of perfectly justifiable steps which he may take to accomplish his desire.

No. 36. SICKNESS—ILL-HEALTH.

- Covered by a heart, the inquirer will suffer from passing ailments, that will leave no bad results.
- Covered by a club, a rather serious illness may be expected.
- Covered by a diamond, an acute attack of a definite disease.
- Covered by a spade, a very severe illness, that may materially interfere with the inquirer's career or happiness.

Tendencies of the Suits.

It will be seen in the foregoing definitions that hearts are almost invariably the sign of good luck, love, and happiness. Even where the position is indicative of misfortune, the presence of a heart has a mitigating effect upon the evil. Clubs rank next in order of good fortune, and seem specially connected with the precious gift of true friendship. Diamonds seem accompanied by the disquieting elements of jealousy and rivalry, which strew obstacles in the path to success and happiness, while for sheer bad luck and dire disaster the ill-omened suit of spades stands unrivalled.

CHAPTER XIV. SIGNIFICATION OF SUITS IN THE MASTER METHOD

COURT CARDS—PLAIN CARDS—AN EXAMPLE OF THE MASTER METHOD.

HEARTS.

THE King of Hearts.—In this method he represents a married man or a widower. Should the inquirer be a woman, and this card fall upon either of the squares, 14, 22, 23, 24, or 32, he then denotes a lover. Should the inquirer be a man, the king falling in the above-named squares signifies a rival.

When this card falls on either of the following numbers, 2, 3, 4, 13, 14, 15, 16, 18, 29, 23, 24, 29, 31, 32, 34, the situation is favourable, and the inquirer will have his wishes granted with respect to the special meaning of the square.

When the king falls on No. 1, 5, 6, 9, 12, 22, 26, 27, or 28, it foretells a satisfactory solution of any matter connected with the subject represented by the squares.

Should he fall upon an unlucky square, namely, No. 7, 8, 10, 11, 27, 20, 22, 30, 33, 35, or 36, he mitigates the evil fortune of the positions.

The Queen of Hearts.—She signifies a married woman or a widow who desires the happiness of the inquirer, and does her best to promote it.

If the inquirer is a man, this card falling on the squares 24, 22, 23, 24, or 32, represents his lady-love. In the event of his being already engaged, his fiancée will possess all the most lovable and desirable qualities.

When the inquirer is a woman, and the queen of hearts falls on either of the above-named squares, it shows that she has a rival to reckon with. Should she be engaged, it indicates that her future husband is both young and well equipped for social and professional success.

When a very elderly person consults the cards, the above combination foretells a peaceful, contented old age.

To any one interested in agriculture, the same combination promises abundant crops.

The Knave of Hearts.—This card represents a good-natured, amiable, but rather insipid young man, devoid alike of violent passions and exalted aspirations.

When a young girl consults the cards, this knave falling on the squares 14, 22, 23, 24, or 32, may be taken to personate her fiancé.

When the inquirer is a young, unmarried man, the same combination indicates that he will marry the object of his choice, after he has surmounted considerable obstacles by his tact and quiet determination.

The Ten of Hearts.—The signification of this card does not differ from that given in the general definitions save in the following cases:—

When it falls on square No. 10, it signifies success.

When it falls on square No. 14, it signifies success in love.

When it falls on square No. 16, it signifies a happy marriage. If, in the last-named case, a knave or a seven falls on No. 7, 15, 17, or 25, there will be several children born of the union.

If the ten of hearts falls on squares 18, 19, 31, or 32, it foretells wealth, intense enjoyment, and real happiness.

The Nine of Hearts.—The only addition to the general signification is, that when this card falls near the seven of clubs, it denotes that a promise already made to the inquirer will shortly be fulfilled.

The Eight of Hearts.—This card is the special messenger of good things when it falls on one of the following squares: 5, 9, 15, 18, 19, 22, or 31.

The Seven of Hearts.—If this card falls on No. 14, 23, 23, 24, or 32, when the inquirer is a bachelor, it signifies that he will very soon take unto himself a wife.

The Two of Hearts.—This is frequently taken as the representative card, and in that case is entirely influenced by its position on the chart, taken in connection with the cards that touch or surround it.

The Ace of Hearts.—This card represents the house of the inquirer as it does in other methods. It is very important to note its position on the chart and its surroundings.

CLUBS.

The King of Clubs.—Taken generally, this card represents a married man or a widower, whose worth as a friend is not to be excelled.

When the inquirer is a young girl, and this king falls on No. 14, 22, 23, 24, or 32, she may rejoice, for she will shortly be united in marriage to the man she loves.

Should a young man be consulting the cards, this king falling on any of the above-named squares denotes a generous, high-minded rival who will meet him in fair fight, and who is far above anything like taking a mean advantage.

When this card falls on No. 18, 19, 20, 27, or 28, it represents the guardian of a minor, whose line of conduct will be determined by the cards which surround or touch it.

The Queen of Clubs.—When a bachelor consults the cards, and this queen falls on No. 14, 22, 23, 24, or 32, it promises him a lady-love whose beauty shall be her strongest attraction.

Should a woman be seeking to know her fate, this queen falling on either of the above-named squares warns her that she has a rival. In the case of the inquirer being a married man or woman, this card represents a woman of high position and great influence who is attractive, to the inquirer, and who will be the means of bringing him or her valuable and pleasing intelligence.

In the case of a business man the above combination denotes that he will be entirely successful in the enterprise which is engrossing all his thoughts at the moment.

The Knave of Clubs.—This card may be taken to represent a sincere and lasting friendship founded upon a basis that will endure.

When the inquirer is a young girl, and this card falls upon either of the matrimonial squares, namely, 14, 22, 23, 24, or 32, it signifies some man who wants to marry her.

In the case of a bachelor, this card on the same squares tells him that he has a rival, either in love or in his business career.

The Ten of Clubs.—This card is the harbinger of good luck if it falls on No. 3, 5, 15, 18, 19, 22, 25, 28, 31, or 32.

Should this card fall on squares 10, 17, or 36, it implies that the inquirer will be asked for a loan in money, which he will be unable to lend.

The Nine of Clubs.—This card means a present, and if it follows a club, the gift will be in money; if it follows a heart, the inquirer may look for a present of jewellery; if it follows a diamond, the gift will be but trifling in value; and if it follows a spade, the recipient of the present will derive no pleasure from it.

The Eight of Clubs has no special significance outside the general definition.

The Seven of Clubs.—This represents a young girl capable of the highest self-devotion, even to risking her life in the interests of the inquirer. The exact nature of her relations and services to the object of her affection will be decided by the surrounding cards.

In the case of a bachelor, this card falling on any of the squares 14, 22, 23, 24, or 32, represents the lady of his choice.

In the case of an unmarried girl or a widow, the same combination points to a generous rival.

Whenever this seven comes out near the nine of hearts, the wish card, it is a token of some signal success for the inquirer.

The Two of Clubs.—This represents the trusted friend of the inquirer, and the square on which it falls will give the requisite information, if its meaning be taken in conjunction with those of the surrounding cards.

The Ace of Clubs.—This card is the sign of a well-ordered life and legitimate hopes, and foretells success in an ordinary career, or the attainment of celebrity in special cases.

Should the inquirer be a soldier by profession, it signifies a fortunate turn of events, that will secure him a rapid rise in the army.

To one interested in agriculture, it promises plentiful crops.

To a traveller, it foretells a most satisfactory result from his journey.

To an actress, it promises phenomenal success in a leading rôle. Should the inquirer or one of his parents be a dramatic or lyrical author, this card is the augury of theatrical success.

DIAMONDS.

The King of Diamonds.—Should the inquirer be a young girl, she will do well to note whether this card falls on any of the matrimonial squares, 14, 22, 23, 24, or 32, for in that case her present admirer is not to be trusted, unless he has cards of good import touching him, or is preceded by either a heart or a club.

The Queen of Diamonds.—If this card falls on any of the matrimonial squares, 14, 22, 23, 24, or 32, it signifies to a bachelor that he will be engaged to one whose character is to be read in the surrounding cards. If this queen be preceded by a heart or a club, it promises good luck on the whole; but if by a diamond or a spade, the augury is bad.

Should the inquirer be a young unmarried woman or a widow, this card falling on the above-named squares indicates that she has a rival whose character is revealed by the cards touching it.

The Knave of Diamonds.—For an unmarried woman or a widow, this card represents a lover from a foreign country. If it is accompanied by a heart, he has many good points to recommend him; if by a club, he is kind and generous; if by a diamond, he is bad-tempered, exacting, and jealous; if by a spade, he is an undesirable, and she had better have nothing to do with him.

The Ten of Diamonds.—The general meaning of this card is a journey.

If it falls between two spades, the journey will be long.

If it falls between two hearts, the journey will be short.

If it falls between two clubs, the journey will be successful.

If it falls between two diamonds, the journey will have bad results.

The Nine of Diamonds.—This card signifies news. If preceded by a heart or a club, the news will be good. If preceded by a diamond or a spade, the news will be bad.

The Eight of Diamonds.—This card signifies a short journey. If it fall between two hearts, the expedition will be an enjoyable pleasure trip.

If between two clubs, it denotes a satisfactory business journey.

If between two diamonds, it signifies a trip begun for pleasure and ending in misadventure.

If between two spades, it signifies an unsuccessful business journey.

The Seven of Diamonds.—This card stands for a young girl of foreign birth and breeding. Taken by itself it means love-sorrows and heart-searchings.

Should the inquirer be a bachelor, and this card fall on one of the matrimonial squares, 14, 22, 23, 24, or 32, it signifies a lady-love as above described.

This seven is an excellent augury when it falls on No. 2, 3, 15, 16, 18, or 27.

The Two of Diamonds has practically the same signification as the deuce of clubs, unless it be selected as the representative card.

The Ace of Diamonds.—The signification of this card is a letter.

If preceded by a heart, it is a letter from a lover or friend.

If preceded by a club, it ist a letter on business or one containing money.

If preceded by a diamond, the letter is dictated by jealousy.

If preceded by a spade, the letter contains bad news.

SPADES.

The King of Spades.—When the inquirer is an unmarried woman or a widow, this card falling on one of the squares, 14, 22, 23, 24, or 32, is indicative of a false lover whose character is mean and base.

When the inquirer is an unmarried man, the above combination signifies that he has a rival.

This card falling on the squares numbered 10, 18, 19, 20, 27, 28, or 29, represents a guardian or the executor of a will.

To a married man, this king is a warning that there are domestic ructions in store for him.

To a married woman, the card cautions her to be very much on her guard when in the society of an attractive but unprincipled man whom she has to meet frequently, and who will bring scandal upon her if she is not most careful.

The Queen of Spades.—When the inquirer is a bachelor, this card falling on No. 14, 22, 23, 24, or 32, represents the lady to whom he will be engaged.

In the case of an unmarried woman or a widow, the combination signifies a rival in love.

The Knave of Spades, the Ten of Spades, the Nine of Spades, and *the Eight of Spades* have no special signification other than that given in the general definitions.

The Seven of Spades.—This card signifies all troubles and worries connected with the tender passion.

Should the inquirer be a man, this seven falling on squares 14, 22, 23, 24, or 32 foretells faithlessness on the part of his *fiancée*, a betrayal of trust by some other woman, or a robbery.

When the inquirer is a woman, this card on any of the same squares points to a rival who will be preferred before her.

The Two of Spades may be taken as a representative card, but otherwise has no special signification.

The Ace of Spades is a card of good omen, meaning perseverance followed by possession, a happy marriage, success, and rapid advancement in business or profession.

An Example of the Master Method.

We have taken the deuce of hearts as the representative card of the inquirer, who is a fair young girl seeking to know her fate. We will give the order in which the thirty-six cards come out, but intend to leave the bulk of them for the reader to solve according to the instructions given.

We have taken the inquirer and her immediate surroundings as an example of the working of the method, and feel sure that any intelligent reader will be able to complete the reading for himself.

- No. 1. Ace of clubs.
- „ 2. Eight of spades.
- „ 3. Two of clubs.
- „ 4. Knave of hearts.
- „ 5. King of diamonds.
- „ 6. King of hearts.
- „ 7. Eight of diamonds.
- „ 8. Ten of clubs.

- No. 9. Ten of hearts.
- „ 10. Seven of spades.
- „ 11. Nine of spades.
- „ 12. Two of spades.
- „ 13. Nine of hearts.
- „ 14. Eight of clubs.
- „ 15. Queen of diamonds.
- „ 16. Two of hearts.

- No. 17. King of spades.
- „ 18. Queen of hearts.
- „ 19. Ace of spades.
- „ 20. Ten of spades.
- „ 21. Knave of spades.

- „ 22. King of clubs.
- „ 23. Nine of clubs.
- „ 24. Eight of hearts.
- „ 25. Queen of clubs.
- „ 26. Knave of diamonds.

- No. 27. Queen of spades.
- „ 28. Seven of diamonds.
- „ 29. Seven of hearts.
- „ 30. Ten of diamonds.
- „ 31. Knave of clubs.
- „ 32. Ace of diamonds.
- „ 33. Ace of hearts.
- „ 34. Seven of clubs.
- „ 35. Two of diamonds.
- „ 36. Nine of diamonds.

We find the inquirer in No. 16, which square when covered by a heart indicates a happy and well-suited marriage. On her left in No. 15 (prosperity) she has the queen of diamonds, a very fair woman who is fond of gossip, and somewhat wanting in refinement of feeling. She will interfere with the inquirer's prosperity through jealousy, but on the whole she will bring good luck because she is preceded by a club. To the right. in No. 17 (sorrow) we have the king of spades, a dark, ambitious, but unscrupulous man, who is the inquirer's legal adviser, and will bring grave sorrow upon her by his underhand dealings. Immediately above her we have in No. 10 (loss) the seven of spades, a card representing troubles connected with a love affair. This square being covered by a spade indicates that she will be unjustly compelled to relinquish her rights, and her chance of marriage may be lessened or postponed by the loss of her fortune.

On the left above her we get in No. 9 (association) the ten of hearts, a most cheering and excellent card, promising her success and happiness in a partnership which she is contemplating. On the right, above, in No. 11 (trouble) we have the nine of spades, a bad omen, signifying the failure of her hopes through the jealousy of some other person.

Immediately below her we find in No. 22 (a gift) the king of clubs, who is her true and valued friend, either a married man or a widower. He will make her a present, and will be actuated by certain motives of self-interest in so doing; but she may keep a good heart, for his presence in that position on the chart indicates that she will soon be united to the man of her choice. On the left, below, in No. 21 (rival) we find the knave of spades, a legal agent whose influence will be instrumental in enabling a rival to triumph over and bring discredit upon the inquirer. On the right, below, we have in No. 23 (a lover) the nine of clubs, which in this case means a gift in money. We may take it that her faithful lover, uninfluenced by her pecuniary losses, has decided to make her a present, probably in the form of marriage settlements.

The remainder of the chart will provide the student with many more interesting particulars regarding the fate of this fair inquirer, and at the same time prove an excellent exercise in the art of cartomancy.

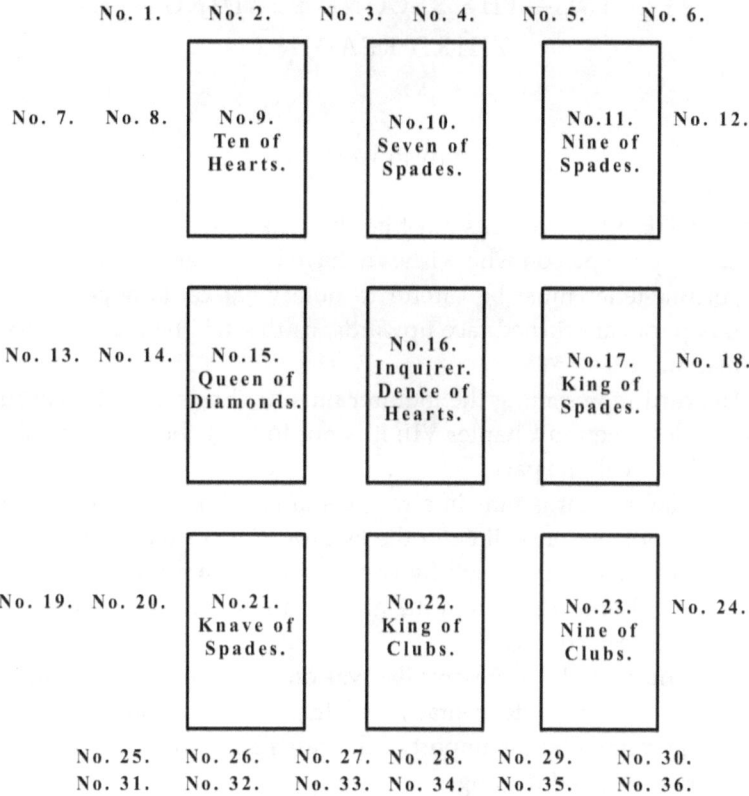

CHAPTER XV. COMBINATION OF NINES

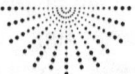

HOW TO WORK IT—AN EXAMPLE—THE FIRST READING—THE SECOND READING—THE THIRD READING

How to Work it.

THE fifty-two cards must be shuffled and cut into three packs by the person who wishes to have his or her fortune told, and the fortune-teller must be careful to note what cards appear as the various packs are turned face upwards, as this will be found to assist the reading.

The card representing the inquirer must first be selected according to the rules given in Chapter VII; it is not to be withdrawn, but shuffled and cut with the pack.

Then lay the cards nine in a row, beginning from right to left with each row; only seven will be in the last row. The cards being in order on the table, you must begin by counting nine from your representative card and nine again from the ninth, until you come to a card that has already been counted.

The court cards represent the various people with whom the inquirer is brought into contact, and their relation and attitude are easily determined by the import of the cards between. Three deals are necessary for a good reading.

An Example.

I give an example of fortune-telling by the combination of nines, because an illustration is of practical help.

The pack having been dealt with in the manner described, we find the cards have resolved themselves thus, reading from left to right in each row:—

First line.—Seven of clubs, seven of spades, king of spades, ace of diamonds, ace of hearts, knave of clubs, four of hearts, eight of hearts, knave of spades.

Second line.—Two of diamonds, three of diamonds, two of hearts, six of hearts, king of diamonds, five of clubs, two of clubs, five of spades, three of hearts.

Third line.—Five of hearts, six of diamonds, four of clubs, queen of clubs, five of diamonds, three of spades, king of hearts, four of diamonds, ten of spades.

Fourth line.—Nine of spades, queen of spades, eight of diamonds, six of clubs, ace of spades, queen of diamonds, king of clubs, knave of hearts, six of spades, nine of hearts.

Fifth line.—Ten of diamonds, eight of clubs, seven of diamonds, ace of clubs, nine of clubs, nine of diamonds, knave of diamonds, ten of hearts, ten of clubs.

Sixth line.—Eight of spades, queen of hearts, seven of hearts, four of spades, three of clubs, two of spades.

We will take the queen of hearts to represent the inquirer, and, as she is in the lowest line of all, will count upwards. The ninth card is the knave of clubs, and the next ninth the six of hearts, then the three of spades, the ace of spades, and nine of clubs, which last brings us back to our queen.

According to the signification given by this method the reading would be as follows

- *Knave of clubs.*—A generous friend.
- *Six of hearts.*—Implies credulity.
- *Three of spades.*—An unfortunate marriage.
- *Ace of spades.*—Difficulties. Be careful in making friends.
- *Nine of clubs.*—Displeasure of friends.

The First Reading.

My general reading of this would be that if the queen of hearts were an unmarried woman she was in danger of making an unhappy marriage, which would bring the displeasure of her friends upon her. If she will avoid forming hasty friendships, and take the advice of a man who is older and darker than herself, she will avoid much misfortune.

If married, the queen is the victim of an ill-assorted union, but she must be careful not to give too much credence to the reports of friends, and must guard her own conduct carefully. We will now proceed with the next deal, to see if we can find a more favourable augury in the Book of Fate.

The Second Reading.

First line.—Eight of clubs, queen of hearts, six of spades, eight of spades, eight of hearts, six of diamonds, ten of hearts, nine of clubs, six of hearts.

Second line.—Three of spades, ace of spades, three of diamonds, king of spades, ace of diamonds, ace of hearts, king of diamonds, king of clubs, ace of clubs.

Third line.—Ten of spades, five of clubs, two of hearts, five of hearts, ten of diamonds, four of hearts, two of clubs, knave of spades, three of hearts.

Fourth line.—Five of spades, four of clubs, six of clubs, queen of diamonds, four of diamonds, king of hearts, nine of spades, five of diamonds, seven of clubs.

Fifth line.—Knave of clubs, ten of clubs, three of clubs, nine of diamonds, queen of spades, seven of spades, knave of hearts, eight of diamonds, seven of diamonds.

Sixth line.—Seven of hearts, four of spades, queen of clubs, two of spades, knave of diamonds, two of diamonds, nine of hearts.

Here our inquirer does not prove to be a very wise person. In spite of the warning and displeasure of friends, regardless of the affection of a good man, and elated through unexpected riches, she listens with credulous mind to one who will cause her much unhappiness. Let us hope she will stop short of one fatal step, and take the good honourable love that is awaiting her.

The ninth card is the king of clubs, and the five of the same suit following in our arranged plan, then the five of diamonds, the ten of clubs, the two of diamonds, the six of hearts, and the three of spades complete this reading. A reference to the signification will show the importance of these cards.

Perhaps in the third reading we may have more success.

The Third Reading.

First line.—Ace of clubs, eight of clubs, queen of hearts, ten of spades, king of clubs, five of diamonds, ten of clubs, nine of spades, knave of spades.

Second line.—Three of spades, two of spades, six of hearts, tight of spades, five of spades, knave of clubs, seven of hearts, four of spades, queen of clubs.

Third line.—Five of hearts, two of diamonds, three of diamonds, queen of diamonds, eight of hearts, three of clubs, five of clubs, ace of diamonds, six of diamonds.

Fourth line.—Four of diamonds, six of clubs, seven of dubs, seven of diamonds, six of spades, nine of diamonds, knave of diamonds, nine of hearts, eight of diamonds.

Fifth line.—Ten of hearts, king of spades, two of hearts, ten of diamonds, ace of hearts, four of hearts, king of hearts, king of diamonds, queen of spades.

Sixth line.—Two of clubs, seven of spades, knave of hearts, nine of clubs, three of hearts, four of clubs, ace of spades.

The cards here are of better promise, though still full of warning. The ninth card is the seven of hearts, which means unfaithfulness, followed by another card indicating domestic dissension. The next is the knave of diamonds, and treachery is to be apprehended. But there is considerable success if care is exercised, and later on there appears to be a happy marriage with comfort and even luxury.

Throughout her life the inquirer would have to be on her guard against forming hasty friendships, and refrain from listening to scandal about those near and dear to her. In this case I should think there would be two marriages, the first not happy (which would probably be dissolved by the law), then a happier time later on in life, with one who had been content to wait.

CHAPTER XVI. YOUR HEART'S DESIRE

THE WISH WITH FIFTEEN CARDS—ANOTHER WAY—THE WISH WITH THIRTY-TWO CARDS—WHAT THE FOUR ACES TELL—THE WISH IN SEVEN PACKS—THE WISH CARD AGAIN.

The Wish with Fifteen Cards.

*H*AVING shuffled the cards well, select according to the second method the card which will represent the inquirer—a king for a man, a queen for a woman—and place this card on the table; then request your subject to wish for some one thing whilst he or she is shuffling the pack (which must only include the selected thirty-two cards). The pack must be cut once.

Take the cards, and holding them easily in your own hands, let the inquirer draw fifteen cards, placing them face downwards on the table, one on top of the other in the order drawn. The fifteen cards having been drawn, discard the others, and place the selected ones in position according to the following plan: The representative card is to be in the centre, and the other cards are to be placed to the left—to the right—above—below—and on the centre, one by one. Thus on the left you will have the first, sixth, and eleventh; on the right, the second, seventh, and twelfth; above, the third, eighth, and thirteenth; below, the fourth, ninth, and fourteenth; and on the representative card you will have placed the fifth, tenth, and fifteenth. (See diagram.)

Then take the left packet and turn and read according to the meaning in the combination of sevens. The next packet to be taken is the one on the right, then the one above, and following that the packet below. The left and top packets represent events that may influence your wish in the future; the packets on the right and below show those events which have influenced it in the past; whilst those cards covering the representative card indicate affairs that may be expected immediately, and are to be read in strict reference to the wish.

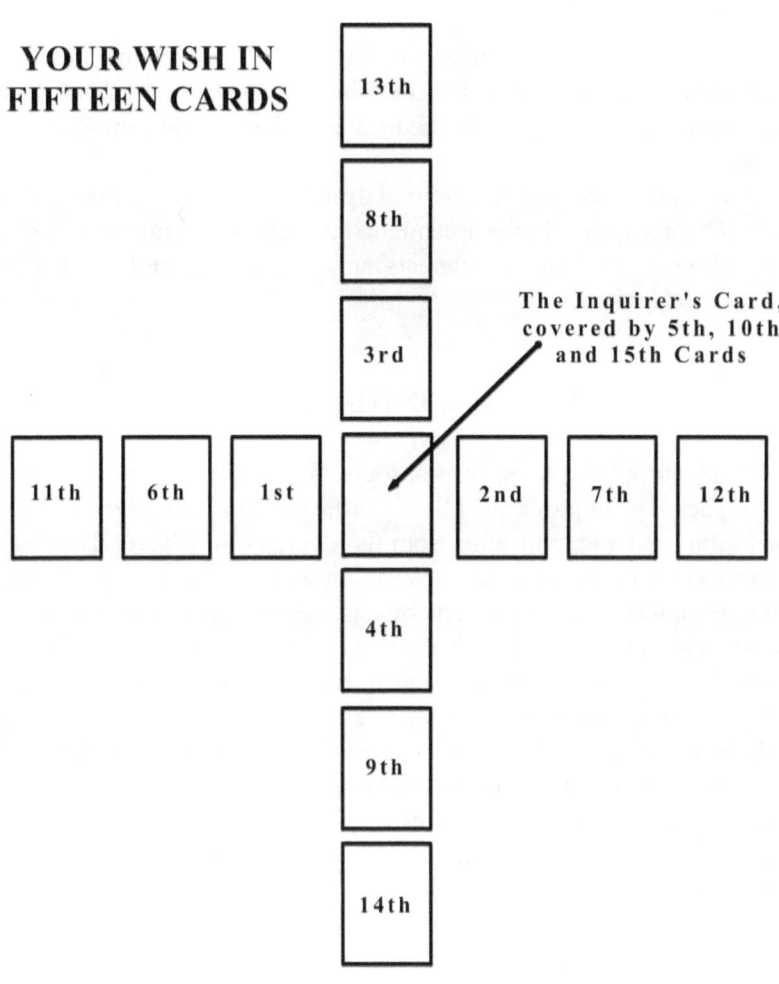

Another Way with Fifty-two Cards.

Let the inquirer shuffle the cards well, and cut them into three packs, having first selected your representative card, as in the former method, and placed it in the centre of a circle.

Take up the packs and lay the cards in a circle, using forty-two, and with the remaining nine form a triangle inside the circle. The cards must be laid face down.

Now let the inquirer choose any fifteen cards, which must be faced upwards as he makes his selection. When fifteen cards are chosen, read the signification according to the meaning given in the combination of nines.

Generally speaking, if diamonds predominate the fortune will be fair; if hearts appear in the ascendant, love affairs are prosperous; clubs will show how material interests are progressing; and spades will prepare us for sorrow.

The Wish with Thirty-two Cards.

Take out all the twos, threes, fours, fives, and sixes from an ordinary pack. The inquirer must then shuffle the remaining thirty-two, cut with the left hand, and wish from the depths of the heart. The dealer places eight cards, face downwards, upon the table in a row before him. He next turns them up one by one, beginning from the left, and as soon as a pair of any kind, it does not matter what, be exposed, they must both be covered by cards taken from the pack in his hand. If they all pair off exactly, it may be taken as a sign that the inquirer's wish will be gratified, but if at any moment there are no pairs exposed, the fates are unpropitious, and the search for a favourable answer must be abandoned. Should most of the cards pair off, leaving only one, two, or three unmated, it portends delay and disappointment before the realisation of the desire.

What the Four Aces Tell.

Take the thirty-two cards up again, shuffle them, and mentally register your wish. The first thirteen cards must be turned up, and a careful search made for any aces that may be there. If found, place them on one side. The rest of the cards must be shuffled again and thirteen more dealt out, with a second search for aces. This is done a third time if all the four have not appeared; and if they still refuse to come, there is no hope of the wish being granted. It is the best possible omen if the four aces come out in the first deal, and very good luck if they arrive with only two attempts; but the third is the last chance, so the turning up of those thirteen cards is fraught with much excitement.

The Wish in Seven Packs.

This is a very simple method, but it is by no means always propitious to the inquirer; if, however, he *does* get the desired answer, we take it that the capricious goddess is in a very smiling mood.

Thirty-two cards are required, and they must be arranged in suits in the following order: Ace, king, queen, knave, ten, nine, eight, seven. The cards must not be shuffled, but the arranged pack is cut, with the left hand, into seven smaller packs, and all are placed face downwards upon the table.

The dealer must then proceed to turn up the top cards of each pack, and as a pair of queens, nines, knaves, or whatever they may happen to be becomes visible, he must remove them from the packs. Should all the cards pair off in this manner, the wish may be taken as one that will speedily be granted. Should the cards come out awkwardly, literally in sixes and sevens instead of pairs, the inquirer must adapt his desires to the inevitable with the best grace he can.

The Wish Card Again.

Yet a sixth way, which will give some idea if the heart's desire will be gratified, is as follows:—

Shuffle the whole pack of cards and give them to the inquirer, who must then divide the pack into three, wishing intently all the time. Take up the packs separately and glance through them; the nine of hearts is the most important card, as that is the symbol of the wish. Should this be in juxtaposition to the card—the king or queen—representing the inquirer, and with favourable surroundings, then you may conclude that the things hoped for will come to pass. Also, if the wish card is in combination with cards that are an indication of the inquirer's desires, it is a favourable augury

For instance, if the wish referred to business, and the suit of clubs surrounded the nine of hearts, then it might be concluded that the matter would terminate in a prosperous manner. Diamonds, as they foretell wealth, would also pro muse prosperity; hearts imply good wishes and good will, whilst spades carry a sinister import.

CHAPTER XVII. A RHYMING DIVINATION

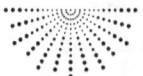

DIAMONDS—HEARTS—SPADES—CLUBS.

THERE are those to whom the more elaborate forms of fortune-telling by cards may seem a trifle wearisome, or possibly too intricate to be followed without a somewhat exhausting effort of attention. The method which we give in this chapter has the advantage of being at once simple, diverting, and varied.

As the rhyming significations concern both sexes, a great deal of fun can be provided where there is a party of young people, and who can tell whether the long arm of coincidence may not use this old-time practice to bring some loving pair together?

Take a new pack of cards, or at any rate one in which there are no tell-tale marks on the reverse sides, and spread them face downwards upon the table. Before any one draws a card, he or she is requested to close the eyes, place the right hand on the heart, and say, "Honi soit qui mal y pense." The card must then be drawn with the left hand, and its meaning will be read by the one who holds the key contained in the verses which we now give.

DIAMONDS.

Ace. Since that this ace is now your lot,
 You will wed one that's fierce and hot;

But if a woman does draw it,
She will wed one with wealth and wit.

Two. Hast thou not drawn the number two?
Thy spouse shall be both just and true.
But if a woman this now have,
Beware a sly and crafty knave!

Three. You that have drawn the number three
Great honour will your fortune be;
But if a female draw the same,
She must beware of fickle shame.

Four. The man that draws the number four
Shall quite forsake his native shore;
But if the same a woman finds,
Both hand and heart in love she joins.

Five. He that draweth the number five,
Where he was born he best will thrive;
But if it's drawn by womankind,
Good luck abroad they sure will find.

Six. He that can catch the number six
Will have cunning and crafty tricks;
But if a woman draw the same,
Twill show that she is free from blame.

Seven. Since that the seven does appear,
Crosses thou hast great cause to fear;
Women, whene'er the same they draw,
Shall not fear crosses more than straw.

Eight. Hast thou then drawn the number eight?
Thou sure wilt be a rascal great;
Females that chance the same to take,
They never will the truth forsake.

Nine. Hast thou turn'd up the merry nine?
Then guineas will thy pocket line;

She that doth draw it to her hand
Will die for love or leave the land.

Ten. O brave! the ten, 'tis very well!
There's none in love shall thee excel.
Only the maid who draws the ten
May wed, but nobody knows when.

King. This noble king of diamonds shows
Thou long shalt live where pleasure flows!
But when a woman draws the king,
Sad, melancholy songs she'll sing.

Queen. Now is the queen of diamonds fair,
She shows thou shalt some office share;
Oh, woman! if it fall to you,
Friends you will have not a few.

Knave. Is now the knave of diamonds come?
Be sure beware the martial drum;
Yet if a woman draw the knave,
She shall much better fortune have.

HEARTS.

Ace. He that draws the ace of hearts
Shall surely be a man of parts;
And she that draws it, I profess,
Will have the gift of idleness.

Two. He who can draw the deuce shall be
Endowed with generosity;
But when a woman draws the card,
It doth betide her cruel hard.

Three. The man who gets hold of this trey
Always bound, always obey;
A woman that shall draw this sort
Will sure drink brandy by the quart.

Four. He that draws this four shall make
A faithful love for conscience' sake;
But if it's drawn by womenkind,
They will prove false, and that you'll find.

Five. Note that this five of hearts declares
Thou shalt well manage great affairs;
But if it's drawn by fair women,
They sure will love all sorts of men.

Six. The six of hearts surely foretells
Thou shalt be where great honour dwells;
If it falls on the other side
It then betokens scorn and pride.

Seven. Now this old seven, I'll maintain,
Shows that thou hast not loved in vain;
Thou shalt obtain the golden prize,
But, with the maids, 'tis otherwise.

Eight. Having drawn the number eight,
Shows thou'rt servile, born to wait;
But if a woman draw the same,
She'll mount upon the wings of fame.

Nine. By this long nine be well assured
The lovesick pains must be endured;
But the maid that draws this nine
Soon in wedlock hands shall join.

Ten. This ten it is a lucky cast,
For it doth show the worst is past;
But if the maids the same shall have,
Love will their tender hearts enslave.

King. By this card surely 'twill appear
Thou shalt live long in happy cheer;
And if a woman draw this card,
She shall likewise be high preferred.

Queen. Now by this card it is well known
Thou shalt enjoy still all thine own;
But women, if they draw the same,
Shall sure enjoy a happy name.

Knave. He that doth draw the knave of hearts
Betokens he hath knavish parts;
But if a woman draw the knave,
Of no man shall she be the slave.

SPADES.

Ace. Thon that dost draw the ace of spades
Shall be sore flouted by the maids;
And when it is a damsel's lot,
Both love and honour go to pot.

Two. Always this deuce betokens strife,
And with a scolding, wicked wife;
But if a woman's lot it be,
Honour, great love, and dignity.

Three. Thou that art happy in this trey
Shalt surely wed a lady gay;
Whilst maids who now the same shall take,
Join marriage with a poor town rake.

Four. Now this same four betokens you
Shall lead a dissipated crew;
Maids that do draw the same shall meet
With certain joys always complete.

Five. The five of spades gives you to know
That you must through some troubles go;
But, if a woman, it foretells
Her virtue others' far excels.

Six. The six foretells whene'er you wed

You'll find your expectations fled;
But if a maid the number own
She'll wed a man of high renown.

Seven. Now as the seven comes to hand,
It does entitle you to land;
But maids with this shall wed with those
That have no money, friends, or clothes.

Eight. This eight of spades foretells you shall
Wed a young maid fair, straight, and tall;
If to a maid the same shall come,
She weds the brother of Tom Thumb.

Nine. Now by this nine thou art foretold,
Thou shalt wed one deaf, lame, and old.
Females, when they draw this odd chance,
Shall of themselves to wealth advance.

Ten. 'Tis seen by this long ten of spades
That thou shalt follow many trades,
And thrive by none. But women, they
By this chance shall not work but play.

King. By this brave king observe and note,
On golden streams you e'er shall float;
But women, by the self-same lot,
Shall long enjoy what they have got.

Queen. Here is the queen of spades, likewise
Thou soon shalt unto riches rise;
A woman by the same shall have
What her own heart doth sorely crave.

Knave. This is a knave, pray have a care
That you fall not into despair;
Women, who the same shall choose,
Shall prove great flats, but that's no news

CLUBS.

Ace. He that doth draw the ace of clubs,
From his wife gets a thousand snubs;
But if maids do it obtain,
It means that they shall rule and reign.

Two. Note that this deuce doth signify
That thou a loyalist shalt die;
The damsels that the same shall take
Never will their good friends forsake.
Three. You that by chance this trey have draws
Shall on a worthless woman fawn.
A maiden that shall draw this trey
Shall be the lass that ne'er says nay.

Four. Now by this four we plainly see
Four children shall be born to thee;
And she that draws the same shall wed
Two wealthy husbands, both well-bred.

Five. Now by this five 'tis clear to see
Thy wife will but a slattern be.
This same five drawn by virgins, they
Shall all wed husbands kind and gay.

Six. By this six thou'rt wed, we know,
To one that over thee will crow;
Maids that can draw the same shall be
Blest with good husbands, kind and free.

Seven. Thou that hast now the seven drawn
Shall put thy Sunday clothes in pawn;
Maids that draw the same shall wear
Jewels rich without compare.

Eight. By this club eight, tho' Whig or Tory,
Thy life will prove a tragic story;
Ye maids that draw the same, are born
To hold both fools and fops in scorn.

Nine. By this brave nine, upon my life,
You soon shall wed a wealthy wife;
She that shall draw the same shall have
One that is both fool and knave.

Ten. Now for this number, half a score,
Shows that thou wilt be wretched poor;
Maids that can draw this number still
Shall have great joy and wealth at will.

King. Here comes the king of clubs, and shows
Thou hast some friends as well as foes;
Maids that do draw this court card shall
Have very few, or none at all.

Queen. If the queen of clubs thou hast,
Thou shalt be with great honour graced.
And women, if the same they find,
Will have things after their own mind.

Knave. See how the surly knave appears!
Pray take care of both your ears!
Women, whene'er the same they see,
Will be what oft they used to be.

CHAPTER XVIII. THE TAROTS

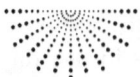

DERIVATION OF NAME—REMOTE ORIGIN— THE GREAT ETTEILLA.

Derivation of Name.

THESE immediate predecessors of our own playing cards were primarily used for divination, and are supposed to have been the invention of one Jacques Gringonneur, an astrologer and cabalist, who was probably of Jewish extraction, as the Tarot packs extant in Europe are of an Israelitish character. Various derivations are given of the name. A simple one is that they were called Tarots because of the crossed diagonal lines upon the back of the cards, a design known by the word *tarotée*. There were Roman numerals in the margin above the symbolic devices. The game played with them after the numeral cards had been added was called *tarrochi*.

Remote Origin.

Cartomancers and occultists trace the Tarots back into the dim and distant past. The science of hieroglyphics was based upon an alphabet in which the gods were letters, the letters were ideas, the ideas numbers, and the numbers perfect signs. This alphabet is supposed to date from the days of Abraham, and is called the famous "Book of Thoth." Moses, who was learned in all the lore of the Egyptians, took it back to his own people and guarded the secret jealously. It is supposed to have come down to us in the Tarots, which have been changed and modified by the time and place of their adoption.

Another theory is given by the famous cartomancer Etteilla, who says: "On a table or altar in the temple of Ptah at Memphis, at the height of the breast of the Egyptian Magus, were, on one side, a book or collection of cards, or plates of gold (the tarots), and on the other a vase, &c." According to this authority the name *tarot* is derived from the pure Egyptian word *Tar*, a path; and *Ro*, *Ros*, *Rog*, royal, the combined meaning reading "The Royal Path of Life."

A writer of the eighteenth century, Count de Gibelen, says: "If it were known that there exists in our day a work of the ancient Egyptians, which had escaped the flames that devoured their superb libraries, and which contains their purest doctrines on the most interesting subjects, every one would doubtless be anxious to acquire the secrets of so valuable a work. . . . This work is composed of seventy-eight illustrations . . ."

Count de Gibelen here refers to the "Book of Thoth," or the Tarot pack of cards. A writer on occult subjects (Macgregor Mathers) believes that the title of this book is derived from *târu*, an Egyptian word which means "to require an answer" or "to consult"; and that the second "t" is added to denote the feminine gender.

"Papus," in his "Key to Occult Science," tells a quaint story as to the reason why the ancient Egyptians came to confide their secrets to the "Book of Thoth." When the overthrow of the kingdom was at hand, the priests met in solemn conclave to decide what means might be used to preserve their secrets inviolate for the initiates of all future ages.

After much deliberation it was held to be best to confide these secrets to something which appealed to vice in man and not to his nobler qualities, so thus the "Book of Thoth" was compiled.

And, indeed, to those interested in occult science it is evident that many solemn mysteries are here symbolised, the explanation of which would be out of place in a book principally designed for amusement, as this is.

The Great Etteilla.

Le Célèbre Etteilla was the great exponent of the mysteries of the Tarots in the time of the French Revolution. He was well known in Paris as a hairdresser, but he had a mind above his trade, and proceeded to steep himself in the study of the occult. Having mastered much of the mystic lore then available, he started to evolve a system of his own, invented mystic signs, made cabalistic calculations, drew diagrams, and produced weighty volumes to further the cause to which he had devoted himself. His principal work appeared in 1783, and from being somewhat of a celebrity as Alliette the fashionable hairdresser, he mounted to the top of the ladder of popular favour, and reigned supreme for thirty years as *Le Célèbre Etteilla*. So much for spelling your name backwards! Disciples and rivals grew up and thronged around him. In the perilous days of 1789, men came to him with blanched lips and drawn features, asking if they might hope to live through the morrow. There were but few "smooth things" to prophesy in those dark days. One cannot help wondering whether he helped any to evade the doom that threatened them.

Etteilla used the Tarots, and adapted them to his own system. Some students of the occult think that he mishandled the sacred emblems of ancient wisdom, but most cartomancers look upon him as one of the chief authorities on fortune-telling by cards, and his method has been made the basis of several subsequent and modern experiments.

It is to be observed that the Tarots are not universally known in the present day, and at the few places where they are sold a fairly high price is asked for them, in comparison with the cost of an ordinary pack of playing cards. For this reason those systems which can only be worked with the Tarots have not been dealt with at length in these pages. The following chapter gives an outline of the way in which these symbolical and mysterious cards can be used, together with some of the significations attached to those composing the major and minor arcana.

CHAPTER XIX. ETTEILLA'S METHOD

THE MAJOR ARCANA—THE MINOR ARCANA—GENERAL RULES—THE SECOND DEAL—THE THIRD DEAL OR GREAT FIGURE—THE FOURTH DEAL.

THE Tarot pack is divided into two parts, called the major and minor arcana, the first consisting of twenty-two cards and the latter of fifty-six, which are again divided into four suits.

We will take first the major arcana, and here we are confronted by some curious figures, each bearing a distinct meaning, typical of man himself and his moral and material life. The first seven cards refer to the intellectual side or mental power of man, the second seven to the moral side, or his attitude towards his fellow-man, whilst the third seven are relative to the various events of his material life. The remaining card is the symbol of the greatest heights it is given to man to reach.

The first step is to learn the actual meaning of each separate card, and remember to which group it belongs.

The Major Arcana.

FIRST.

- The Juggler.—Male inquirer.
- High Priestess.—Woman.
- Empress.—Action; initiative.
- Emperor.—Will.
- Pope or Priest.—Inspiration.

- Lovers.—Love.
- Chariot.—Triumph; Providential protection.

SECOND.

- Justice.—Justice.
- The Hermit.—Prudence.
- The Wheel of Fortune.—Destiny.
- Strength.—Fortitude; courage.
- The Hanged Man.—Trial or sacrifice.
- Death.—Death.
- Temperance.—Temperance.

THIRD.

- The Devil.—Immense force or illness.
- The Struck Tower.—Ruin and deception.
- The Stars.—Hope.
- Moon.—Hidden enemies; danger.
- Sun.—Material happiness; marriage.
- Judgment.—Change of position.
- The Foolish Man.—Inconsiderate actions.
- The Universe.—Success.

The Minor Arcana.

This consists of four suits, known as sceptres, cups, swords, and pentacles, which correspond to the four suits of the pack of playing cards in general use. Each suit also bears a symbolical meaning, which I give—

- Sceptres correspond to diamonds, and mean enterprise.
- Cups correspond to hearts , and mean love.
- Swords correspond to spades , and mean misfortune.
- Pentacles correspond to clubs , and mean interest.

The court cards consist of king, queen, knight, and knave, and represent respectively man, woman, youth, and childhood. These also have another meaning, which is interesting—

- King.— Divine world (spirituality).
- Queen.—Human world (vitality).
- Knight.—Material world (materiality).
- Knave.—Transition stage, *i.e.* life passed on.

The remaining cards in each suit count from one to ten inclusively, and these must be considered in relation to the suit and their face value. "Papus," in his "Key to Occult Science," has given a few suggestions which considerably simplify fortune-telling with the Tarot pack.

By dividing the ten cards of each suit into four sets, we get the relation which they bear to the court cards. The first three, 1, 2, 3, relate to man, which signifies creation and enterprise. The second division, 4, 5, 6, pertain to woman, in opposition to man, that is, reflection and negation. The third division, 7, 8, 9, represent youth and materialism, whilst the ten in each suit makes the fourth set, and relates to the knave or childhood, a transitory or neuter period.

Having thoroughly studied the meaning of each section and each card, it is now necessary to consider some of the methods of divination.

General Rules.

As stated in the preceding chapter, Etteilla, the famous cartomancer, used the Tarot pack, and we can scarcely do better than follow his general rules and method.

The whole pack of seventy-eight cards is to be shuffled and cut into three packs, each consisting of twenty-six cards. Take the centre pack and place it to the right. Then the inquirer must again shuffle the remaining cards and divide into three packs of seventeen cards. Take again the centre pack and place on the right hand, keeping it separate, however, from the first. Another shuffle, and again cut into three packs of eleven cards each, and take the centre pack.

Before proceeding further, it is necessary to explain what to do with the cards that are over. 78 will divide into three times 26 evenly;

but three times 17 = 51, therefore there is one card over. This card is to be shuffled with the pack for the third time, and when cut there will be found two over, which two cards must remain as a discard until the centre pack of eleven has been selected. There will now be three packs of cards on the right hand—one of twenty-six, one of seventeen, and one of eleven; the discard will consist of twenty-four cards.

Take the first pack of 26 and draw off each card separately, laying it on the table from right to left. The second and third packs must be dealt with in similar fashion, only placing them under the first, thus—

26
17
11

The cards being placed, and the signification of each card being kept in mind, the reading can be given. In this figure the lowest line refers to the body or material needs of the inquirer; the second or middle line to the minds or to the affairs on which the thoughts are more specially directed; and the upper line to the unseen or spiritual sense.

The Second Deal.

Shuffle the whole pack and let the inquirer cut once. Then draw off the first seventeen cards, and look at the eighteenth and also at the last card in the pack. These two cards will show you if you have established any sympathy between yourself and the inquirer—a fact which must be judged from the signification the cards bear to the inquirer.

Lay out the seventeen cards selected, and place them in order from right to left, then give the interpretation. Pair, by taking the 1st and the 17th, 2nd and 16th, and so on to the end. The pairing should either enhance or modify the deductions already drawn.

The Third Deal or Great Figure.

This method is more elaborate than any of the others. Let all the cards be well shuffled and cut by the inquirer, then arrange in the following order:—

On your right hand, working upwards, place eleven cards.

Opposite to the first card, but leaving a space between (see diagram), place the 12th card, and work upwards from that until you have arranged another column of eleven cards.

From the 11th card on the right, begin and place eleven cards across, which arrangement will give you the three sides of a square formed by thirty-three cards. Then form the circle by commencing with the 34th card, and placing it in a line with the centre card of the top row. Sixty-six cards will now have been used. One card must represent the inquirer, and should be placed in the centre, and the more satisfactory plan is to take the juggler to represent a man, and the high priestess a woman, instead of simply drawing any card by chance. Eleven cards now remain, and with these the triangle inside the circle can be formed. The apex of the triangle will be towards the manipulator, as shown in the diagram.

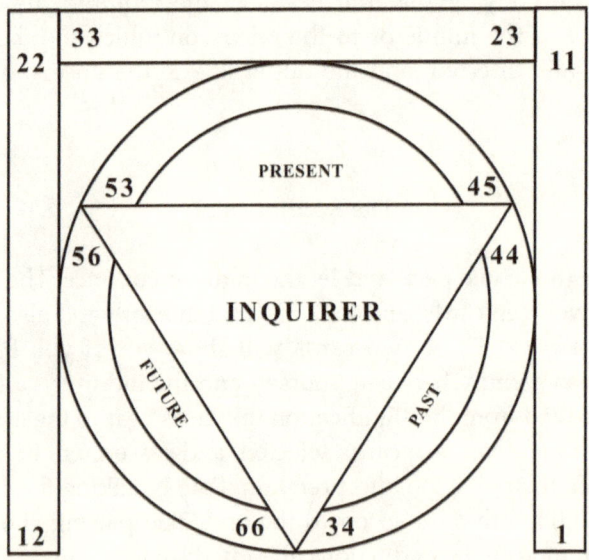

This figure will give a reading of the past, present, and future—the right referring to the events that have passed, the left to things as they are at present known, and the third to what is to come.

The first card placed on the square and the first card placed on the circle are paired, then the 2nd and the 35th, the 3rd and 36th, and so on until you have taken all the cards on the right, which will give you a reading of the past. Pair the 23rd card with the 45th, and proceed until you have finished with the section referring to the present.

For the future, take the 12th card and the 66th, and read the indication of events to come.

The triangle formed of the eleven cards is an innovation on Etteilla's method, but, read in reference to the deductions made, it will probably confirm the cartomancer's opinions. This figure requires much attention and patience, especially if the more symbolical meaning of the cards is studied.

The Fourth Deal.

This refers only to the wish. Let the inquirer shuffle the cards, then draw off the first seven and lay them from right to left, and read according to the meaning.

Copyright © 2020 by Alicia Editions
Credits: CANVA, Wikipedia Commons.
All rights reserved.
No part of this book may be reproduced in any form or by any electronic or mechanical means, including information storage and retrieval systems, without written permission from the author, except for the use of brief quotations in a book review.

www.ingramcontent.com/pod-product-compliance
Lightning Source LLC
LaVergne TN
LVHW040105080526
838202LV00045B/3787